The Little Book of
Sanuk

The Little Book of
Sanuk

The Thai Secret to a
More Joyful Life

 Karen Sinotok

HarperCollins*Publishers*
1 London Bridge Street
London SE1 9GF

www.harpercollins.co.uk

HarperCollins*Publishers*
Macken House, 39/40 Mayor Street Upper
Dublin 1, D01 C9W8, Ireland

First published by HarperCollins*Publishers* 2024

1 3 5 7 9 10 8 6 4 2

© Karen Sinotok 2024

Illustrations © Ploypisut 2024

Karen Sinotok asserts the moral right to be identified as the author of this work

A catalogue record of this book is available from the British Library

ISBN 978-0-00-865781-9

Printed and bound at PNB, Latvia

This book is produced from independently certified FSC™ paper to ensure responsible forest management.

For more information visit: www.harpercollins.co.uk/green

Contents

Sanuk (san-ook)

1. *verb* Enjoy; be enjoyable; have a good time; be funny

2. *adjective* Pleasant; funny; fun; entertaining; amusing; vivacious; diverting; enjoyable

Introduction

When was the last time you had fun? Perhaps it was a catch-up with old friends over dinner as you retold familiar stories which still bring tears of laughter to your eyes. Or maybe it was playing with your kids, giggling with a colleague over a work in-joke, singing along at a concert or helping neighbours to make your community a better place to live.

Whatever the occasion, chances are it sparked a feeling in you that you'd like to experience a lot more of. The joy of being totally in the moment and free from anxiety is a magical state when we feel truly alive. But what if you could bring that feeling of lightness into your life ovory day?

Sanuk is a Thai concept that can loosely be translated as meaning 'fun', though sanuk is, in fact, much more than that – it's about achieving pleasure, satisfaction and togetherness in all aspects of life. It's a happier, more optimistic way of living, and it's something we can all learn to embrace.

Deeply ingrained in Thai culture, sanuk is a guiding principle in Thai people's day-to-day lives. Everything should be as enjoyable as possible. Nothing is taken too seriously, and anything worth doing should contain some element of sanuk.

In Thailand, fun is more than a simple noun or adjective. It is a way of life, rooted in the culture of sanuk. A 2018 report for Visa explained sanuk like this:

> **Whilst every culture has a word for 'fun', in Thailand, sanuk is elevated to an ethos, a way of life that intrinsically permeates how Thais think about and do things, almost to the extent that 'If it's not sanuk, it's not worth doing'. Thais infuse everyday moments with fun, be it by gentle teasing or playful bantering with others. Communal spaces such as markets and street food stalls facilitate social interactions where sanuk happens.**

I love this description!

You know sanuk when you feel it, and Thai people believe that it's the little things that add up to a joyful life. Whether it's spending time with friends and family, raising happy children or having a laugh with colleagues, they always try to bring a sense of fun into their daily routines. It's the easy-going, fun-loving way of life that Thai people strive to lead, and it's the reason why Thailand is known as the Land of Smiles.

In search of sanuk

I've been married to Sit, a Thai man, for 30 years, and we've split our time between the UK and Thailand as we've raised our son, Siam. With intimate knowledge of how real Thai families live and work, I've seen many examples of sanuk in Thai people's day-to-day lives. I've learned from personal experience that the Thai way of life has much to teach us. We can all bring more happiness into our lives by adopting the positivity of sanuk.

It all started in 1993, when I decided to take a very belated gap-year trip …

After a career as a pop-music journalist which saw me partying with George Michael, interviewing David Bowie and travelling the world with the biggest bands of the day, I returned to the UK from a stint in New York and joined a top-selling consumer magazine as a senior editor.

Fast forward a few years, and I found myself well paid, but desk-bound, stressed out and living on cigarettes and Diet Coke. I knew I was tired of the daily grind, but what I didn't know at the time was that I was in search of sanuk – a way to bring some fun back into my life.

Keen for a complete change of scenery, and some much-needed winter sun, I booked a two-week trip with a friend to Thailand. I'd never been to Asia before, so wasn't completely sure what to expect, but I'd seen enough travel-agent posters of deserted white-sand beaches and azure seas to know that it would be an improvement on England in February.

That holiday made the choice for me.

The heat, the food, the people, those beaches … just wow! On my return, London had never looked greyer, or my office less appealing. So I made a big decision. Much to the bemusement (and amusement) of my metropolitan media friends, I took a career break. I handed in my notice, sold off my designer outfits and, with the proceeds, I bought a round-the-world ticket. Then I threw some shorts, T-shirts and mosquito repellant into a backpack and headed East.

Like countless Westerners before and since, I was looking for something more. I wanted adventure, a taste of freedom – plus a bit of the sunshine lifestyle that seemed to make everyone who lived there so darned serene and happy.

My trip through Southeast Asia ground to a halt eight months later on Thong Nai Pan Noi, a small, jaw-droppingly beautiful bay in the northwest of the (then) unspoiled Thai island of Koh Pha Ngan. After a two-day journey overland from Bangkok, perched in the back of an ancient pick-up truck, tired, dust-covered and gasping for a cold

My paradise found: Thong Nai Pan Noi

As starter homes go, it was basic!

The Little Book of Sanuk

Singha beer, I'd finally reached my destination. As we bumped our way round the final corner of the dirt road, it was love at first sight. I gleefully ticked off my mental checklist: white-sand beach, CHECK; azure sea, CHECK; a few groups of wooden beach huts, framed by coconut trees with brightly coloured, tie-dye hammocks slung between them, OH YES! I'd found my sun-drenched nirvana.

My travelling days on pause, it wasn't long before I had another reason to stay; I soon met Sit, a fun-loving Thai hippy, who was running a beachside bungalow resort called Bio's Dynamic Kitchen, which served a delicious three-course Thai dinner every night for the equivalent of a takeaway coffee back in London. He built a simple bamboo tree hut with a leaky leaf roof for the two of us, where we lived in a shifting beach community of travellers from around the world and an ever-changing group of long-haired, guitar-playing Thai workers who serenaded us in the evenings. We swam in the sea, drank chilled, fresh coconut water on the beach, listened to a *lot* of Bob Marley, read books and dozed in hammocks.

I'd never had so little in the way of possessions but had never been happier. Whether it was playing raucous card games with new friends, exploring the island on the back of a motorbike or creating mobiles from shells to decorate our hut (as starter homes go, it was on the basic end of the spectrum), every day was sanuk.

But it was a visit to Sit's family and friends in his home city of Bangkok a few months later that showed me another side to the country I'd fallen so hard for. It wasn't just us lucky souls hanging out on a beautiful beach with no job to get up for in the morning who'd been finding joy in the everyday; creating good times is embedded in Thai culture. Despite the language barrier, Sit's relatives immediately welcomed me into the family and a home filled with laughter. We all had fun trying to communicate as they showed me the sights, took me on shopping trips and fun nights out. I even found myself at a karaoke club, something so unlike me, but the spirit of sanuk was strong.

The spirit of Songkran

By coincidence, my first trip to the capital coincided with Songkran, aka the Water Festival – the traditional Thai new-year celebration in April. A combination of the spiritual and slapstick, every year, for three days, normal life in one of the busiest cities in the world grinds to a halt for a giant water fight. The streets were thronged with people and drenched in water, but everyone was laughing and smiling, including me. This was peak sanuk.

Songkran sums up the Thai attitude to life, with loved ones at its centre. As their Buddhist beliefs mean they don't celebrate Christmas,

SANUK TIP
Once the party's over,
and daily life resumes,
Thai people do their best to
ensure that the fun continues.
Follow their example and
live as if every day
is a holiday.

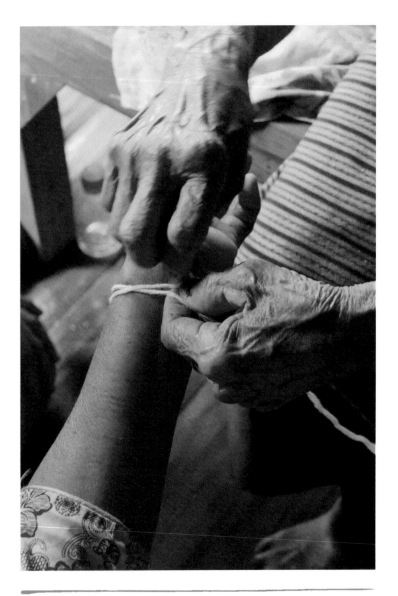

The Little Book of Sanuk

Songkran is the time when Thai families come together from around the country to reunite in their hometowns. It takes place in the hottest month, when temperatures often soar to a sweltering 35°C or higher, so on a purely practical level, it's a great way to cool down. But there's also a much deeper significance to Songkran. It embodies not only the Thais' sanuk attitude, but also the essential caring and unity at the core of their society.

Along with Sit's brother Meuk, sister Jim, her husband, Toy, and their three young daughters June, Jan and Joy, we headed to his dad's hometown of Ban Pho, an hour or so outside Bangkok. Everyone dressed up in their brightest clothes, with even the most conservatively clad dads donning lurid flowery shirts. While the person with the biggest house tends to be the main host, everyone provides food and drink, and we staggered in carrying enough provisions to feed a village, as well as offerings for the monks in the local temple.

The younger members of Sit's family lined up to pour water over the hands and feet of the older people as a show of respect, as well as representing the washing away of bad luck. In return, the kids were given blessings and floral garlands. White strings are also tied to one another's wrist for good luck.

Another part of the tradition is to apply a white powder made into a paste (din sor pong) on each other, which is said to ward off bad luck. At the house, this was dabbed in gentle stripes on the forehead and cheeks, but the applications seemed to get clumsier and messier as the day (and alcohol consumed by city revellers) went on, so that by nighttime, most of the faces we saw on our journey home were so smeared in white they were completely covered.

The public street celebrations offer a chance for kids and teenagers (as well as those old enough to know better) to indulge in a little

Three reasons why Songkran is ultimate sanuk

1.

Street stalls spring up selling giant brightly coloured water guns to adults, while major roads are closed to traffic and used as arenas for water fights.

2.

Pick-up trucks packed with laughing groups of people roam towns and cities, spraying passers-by with water from buckets, water cannons and hosepipes.

3.

Smartly dressed office workers tolerate being soaked with ice-cold water on their way to the office.

raucous sanuk, and over the days that followed, I discovered that there's something very liberating about blasting passers-by with jets of water. Everyone can enjoy playing at being kids again.

But while it's three days of wet and wild anarchy, things don't turn violent. For Western observers, it's a source of constant amazement that the festival passes off peacefully every year; it's hard to imagine something similar happening on Britain's city streets without some kind of trouble kicking off. And that is partly down to the Buddhist faith – the peace-loving religion of choice for most Thais. But it also has lots to do with the spirit of sanuk – the sense of fun, combined with the philosophy of putting the happiness of others first and keeping a cool head.

Dream destination

Songkran is just one of the many, many reasons I love Thailand. As well as the welcoming people and delicious food, its tropical islands and steamy rainforests make it simply the most beautiful place I've ever been. I'm not alone in falling for its charms. Since the first wave of adventurous nineteenth century explorers visiting what was then known as Siam, this beautiful Southeast Asian country has been a magnet for travellers, Bangkok being the most visited city in the world, with around 22.8 million visitors in 2023.

It was the 1960s which really put Thailand on the Western radar, as part of the alternative hippie trail from London through Asia for those seeking freedom, spiritual enlightenment and an escape from the strait-laced nine-to-five expectations of home.

Younger readers will find it hard to imagine how on earth anyone ever managed to share information pre-Internet, but share it they did.

The best beaches to visit, the food stall selling amazing noodle soup, the overnight bus which *didn't* stop off at the driver's cousin's sapphire factory en route … news of all this and more spread by word of mouth. People swapped trip highs and lows with others they met along the way. The message boards in cheap guest houses turned into a kind of Hip(pie) Advisor with constantly updated personal recommendations and reviews.

As these freedom-loving travellers often stayed for months, and hung out with locals, their advice was worth listening to. Then, with the launch of the Lonely Planet guidebooks in 1973, full of insider tips and honest reviews, backpackers like me who followed on their heels had their go-to bible … More than just a book, Lonely Planet was an engaging travel companion, as well as an icebreaker when solo dining. It's still a lingering regret that I gave away my battered 1993 copy, full of scribbled notes in the margins, to a random German tourist I struck up a conversation with over breakfast as I was leaving the country on a trip back to the UK.

Now, with Trip Advisor containing over 7 million reviews (7,146,632 last time I checked) on all things Thai, from temples and islands, to tours, restaurants and hotels, there's never been more interest in this tropical paradise.

As one of the easiest places to travel in Asia, Thailand has also become the first stop for gap-year British backpackers, as well as one of the top long-haul destinations for their sun-seeking parents and grandparents, with nearly 40 million tourists visiting a year pre-COVID. With the end of pandemic travel restrictions, the country's tourism sector bounced back, with 22.2 million international visitors in 2023. They go for the sunshine and amazing food but, like me, they return raving about the people and their laid-back lifestyle.

So what can Thai culture teach us?

The strong social connections fostered by the spirit of sanuk mean it has clear psychological benefits for wellbeing. And that is something we have never needed more.

We are currently in the midst of a worldwide mental-health crisis. UK statistics alone make for sober reading: a little over 1 in 10 of the population will be living with an anxiety disorder at any one time – that's over 8 million people; and in a snapshot of national wellbeing in August 2023 by the Office for National Statistics (ONS), nearly 1 in 10 adults (9.2 per cent) reported low levels of happiness.

The World Health Organization's recent review of world mental health found that in 2019, nearly a billion people – including 14 per cent of the world's adolescents – were living with a mental disorder. It's a global problem which COVID-19 exacerbated. The WHO reported in 2022 that depression and anxiety went up by more than 25 per cent in the first year of the pandemic alone.

We cannot create a society without stress, but sanuk can help to counter today's anxiety epidemic by helping to reframe the way we approach life and cope with its challenges. Sanuk acknowledges that bad things can happen but encourages a sense of resilience that helps Thais bounce back from adversity. Those smiling schoolboy footballers rescued after being trapped in a cave in northern Thailand for two weeks in 2018 are examples of how this can help people cope in the toughest

> **Don't seize the day. Just tickle its belly.**
>
> Thai proverb

of times. And, if the worst happens, having a sense of togetherness provides a support system when it comes to dealing with hardships and helping people through loss and grief.

It's hardly breaking news that we in the West have material wealth but have never been unhappier or more stressed out. Study after study shows that happiness depends on good health and friends, not money. In fact, people have become no happier in the last 50 years, despite average incomes more than doubling. So if money can't buy happiness, what's the solution?

I believe it's time for a reminder that joy and fun can be found in *all* elements of life. We all need to bring more pleasure into our lives by reconnecting with loved ones, embracing new connections and coming together to help make the world a better place, one smile at a time.

In this book I'll show how everyone can inject sanuk into all aspects of their lives. From raising happier children to learning how to connect more with those around us and the world we live in, I will be drawing on the latest research to share simple ways we can all be happier. And because food with loved ones is ultimate sanuk, I'll be sharing a couple of authentic, delicious recipes which Thai people cook to eat with friends and family, too.

The warmth of Thailand is reflected in the personalities of its people, and while we may not have their tropical climate, there are many lessons we can learn from them. In a time of global turbulence, it's never been more important to make the most of every minute and find pleasure in the everyday. This book aims to capture that happy positive mood and show how we can all get a year-round post-holiday buzz or create it in our own lives without leaving our postcode; I hope it will help you find ways to live in the moment and have some sanuk of your own.

The sanuk dictionary

JAI DII – Good heart; to be told that you possess jai dii is a great compliment.

JAI YEN – Cool heart; a heart characterised by composure, calm and patience – keeping cool in tense situations is an ability that is prized in Thai society.

JAI YEN YEN – Calm down; take it easy; don't get angrier; don't get so excited; also, don't be nervous or in such a hurry to do something.

KAO JAI – I understand (literally, to enter the heart).

KRENG JAI – Consideration for others; this can blend with sanuk, leading to a sense of community – helps to maintain harmonious relationships and promote a sense of collective wellbeing.

KWAAM SUK – Happiness.

MAI ME PEN HA – No problem; a response when someone is grateful for something you've done.

MAI MUN MAI TUM – If it's not fun, I won't do it.

MAI PEN RAI – No worries; it's ok; don't worry; it doesn't matter; never mind (one of the most-used phrases in the Thai language, these three words can be used for moments big and small).

SANUK MAI – Are you having fun?

1.

Are You Having Fun?

- Sanuk Mai

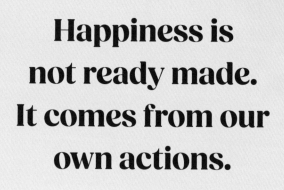

Happiness is not ready made. It comes from our own actions.

Thai proverb

When I'm out and about with Thai family and friends, they like to check to see if I'm having a good time. Whatever the occasion, they'll ask: 'Sanuk mai?' – basically, 'Are you having fun?' The only acceptable answer, by the way, is: 'Sanuk!' I could, of course, say 'Mai sanuk' ('Nope, not having fun'), but the disappointed looks on their faces from such a response would haunt me for the rest of my days …

Thai people never pass up an opportunity to enjoy themselves, so when making choices in their lives, sanuk is a factor: some pleasure must be combined with whatever they do. And when life is lacking sanuk, they'll plan it. (They literally don't understand the concept of Fear Of Missing Out – FOMO.) If you wanted a song to sum up their philosophy, it would be 'Don't Worry Be Happy' by Bobby McFerrin.

As far as the Thais are concerned, activities that are otherwise dull and monotonous should be spiced up with a little playfulness. It's about imbuing ordinary moments with a fun twist. One Thai friend summed it up, saying, 'Sanuk is a state of mind. You choose to be happy. We believe in this concept so much that we try to live our life by it. If it isn't fun, then don't do it!'

If that sounds frivolous or shallow, it isn't. At a time when so many of us have lost our connection to fun, it's never been more important to seize moments of joy and bring more pleasure to our everyday lives where and when we can. In a world of rolling news and information overload, which can send even the most well-adjusted of us into an impotent spiral of despair, this is a refreshing alternative. By embracing the spirit of sanuk, we can release ourselves from the drudgery of hamster-wheel life and make things less stressful and more fun.

Planning for fun

The impact of the pandemic on the mental health and wellbeing of us all has been huge. That's why we need to look at what brings us joy, so that we can actively try to create more playfulness and spontaneity in our lives.

And if you think it's impossible to plan for fun, try this: cast your mind back to when you last had the best time. Think about who you were with and make an effort to meet up with them; consider what you were doing and schedule that activity. It really can be that simple.

In fact, the delicious thrill of anticipation can be as much fun as the event itself. Kids are masters at this; anyone who's spent time with a child under 10 in the weeks before Christmas knows that looking forward to the big day is all a big part of the excitement. Looking ahead brings more joy than looking back, with one study into the connection between anticipation and happiness finding that when it comes to holidays, just planning or being excited about your trip can make you happier than actually taking it.

Of course, it's easy to let day-to-day commitments get in the way of planning for fun. As I sat at my laptop, working long days to hit my deadline for this book, I found myself turning down invitations and generally becoming a stay-at-home grouch.

The irony of it struck me after a few weeks; how absurd not to practise what I was preaching! So I made a conscious decision to take time out. I'd arrange coffee with a mate who makes me laugh, go for a solo spin along the coast on my e-bike (the sanuk way to cycle) or see if Sit fancied a quick game of tennis (we're both terrible, which makes it more fun). I'd return to my desk refreshed and inspired. Every. Single. Time. There's no better way to remind yourself of the benefits that taking a break brings than to take one.

The ways in which we self-sabotage are familiar to clinical psychologist Dr Jessamy Hibberd, whose area of expertise is adult mental health. She believes we need to learn to prioritise pleasurable activities: 'Not all time needs to be productive. It's important to do things just for fun, with no expected outcome or greater purpose than enjoying yourself. As kids we know the importance of fun, but somewhere along the line it gets lost as we go into adulthood and moved down the priority list. Play is important for happiness and creativity and is something we should actively keep in our lives.'

Studies have found some of the reasons why having a good time for its own sake can improve our emotional wellbeing. When we do pleasurable activities, it releases the feel-good hormone dopamine which boosts positivity and can counteract feelings of hopelessness and stress. Doing fun stuff also provides a source of something called eustress – a type of positive stress that can contribute to feelings of optimism and excitement about life.

There are physical benefits, too. Research by Professor Matthew Zawadzki, a health psychologist with the University of California Merced, showed that when people engage in leisure activity, they have a lower heart rate and more psychological engagement – that means less boredom, which can help to avoid unhealthy behaviours.

Having fun also allows us the opportunity to connect and create bonds with others – one of the key drivers when it comes to sanuk.

Four ways to
kickstart good times

1.

Make a list. Write down activities you enjoy or want to try – hobbies, sports, crafts, outdoor adventures, social get togethers or cultural trips – whatever puts a smile on your face.

2.

Commit. When will you be able to fit these things into your life? Take an honest look at your schedule and block out some time.

3.

Invite people along. Boost sanuk and create lasting memories by sharing experiences with others. They'll also help to hold you accountable and ensure the fun actually happens.

4.

Make reservations. Sign up for something that involves a non-refundable deposit and you'll automatically be more committed.

Sanuk showgirls

Ladyboys, or kathoeys, have a unique history and culture in Thailand. With a tradition of tolerance, they are widely accepted by Thai society, and have broken out of the stereotypes to become pop stars, models, actors and even politicians. Their cabaret shows can be spectacularly sanuk – a mix of song and dance and fun slapstick comedy.

When we lived in Koh Samui the stunning transgender stars of the island's show would stay in shape by playing volleyball on our local beach every afternoon. Watching this was a lot of fun, mainly as they put on such a sanuk show – naked except for thongs! They looked beautiful, but there was nothing delicate about the way they played … woe betide the brave Westerner who tried to join in.

The past is already gone; the future is not yet here. There's only one moment for you to live, and that is the present moment.

Buddha

Living in the moment

When the pandemic swept across the planet in 2020, leaving us confined to home and unable to socialise or see loved ones, it created an environment which was the very antithesis of sanuk. This fierce wake-up call reminded us not just how precious life is, but also how crucial human connections are. We've all emerged more fragile, and keen to make up for lost time when it comes to experiencing and enjoying life. We've realised that we need to seize the day and make the most of every moment.

Even before we'd ever heard of COVID-19, a poll by Helly Hanson in 2016 found that the average Brit considered less than a third of their day to be enjoyable. One in 10 said they were completely missing fun from their lives.

The spirit of sanuk can literally transform your life. You can live longer, have better health, become happier and less stressed. Happy to live in the moment, Thai people don't stress about the future and don't worry about tomorrow. They find joy in simple pleasures and appreciate what they have in the here and now, rather than constantly pushing for more. For Westerners caught up in a culture of constantly striving for the next thing, then feeling unhappy when we don't get it, or dissatisfied when we do, making this mind shift has clear mental-health benefits.

Noel McDermott is a British psychotherapist with over 25 years' experience in health, social care and education. He says that when we are more mindful of what's going on in the moment, our happiness levels will rise.

'We forget to live in the moment as we get older,' explains Noel. 'It's too easy to forget to enjoy what you have right now. Don't get caught up in events that have not yet occurred, don't allow yourself to dwell too much on the challenges that lie ahead. Live in the here and now, focus your mind and make decisions about what you choose to dwell on. Let go of what you don't need to or can't control and learn to be in the flow of things more. Ask yourself, is this moment bad or is something else bad? When you are more mindful, you can realise that most of the moments are fine.'

The best things in life are free

You can't put a price tag on fun, and Thai people know innately what studies confirm – that you can have a happy life even if you don't have a lot of money. Thailand ranks just 78th in the International Monetary Fund 2023's richest countries in the world, but having a limited budget can actually increase opportunities for sanuk because it encourages human connection over possessions.

We've known for a long time that the stuff that we *do* has more substantial long-term benefits than the stuff we buy, despite our consumer-driven society. Research shows that experiential purchases, such as lunch with friends or a family weekend away, are more likely to boost our happiness than buying a new outfit, or even a car, where the dopamine hit gives us a short-lived buzz. Why is this? Well, it's all down to something called hedonic habituation: our brains quickly readjust to the new normal, and our shiny new purchase soon loses its ability to spark joy. We, meanwhile, return to our usual baseline of happiness. Experiences are different, though: the benefits linger on so much that even the memory of a fun time can boost our moods.

10 *free* ways to have fun

1.
Head to your nearest park with a pal (or 10), a ball and a frisbee.

2.
Host a games night with board games, cards, trivia quizzes.

3.
Invite friends over for dinner, where everyone brings a dish.

4.
Organise a clothes swap with your friends.

5.
Check out a new neighbourhood.

6.
Make a time capsule of things which sum up life as it is right now.

7.
Have a mini spa day with friends with DIY facials, manicures, massages.

8.
Offer to walk a neighbour's dog.

9.
Have a culture day – visit your local free museum, watch a classic movie.

10.
Exchange homes for a night with friends who live somewhere completely different.

Be a glass-half-full person

Sanuk doesn't just help us to enjoy life more. In a growing field of medical research, recent ground-breaking studies are showing a clear link between a person's outlook on life and their health. A mindset of optimism and positivity has obvious benefits. Being a glass-half-full person doesn't just help us live longer; it helps us live *better*. In essence, optimists have fewer strokes, sleep better and have a better quality of life than pessimists.

So how do you change your outlook?

First, it pays to be aware that human instincts have been shaped over millennia, and fearing the worst is partly an evolutionary hangover.

'Humans are born with the capacity to look for problems,' explains Noel McDermott. 'Historically, this has been a good thing; our ancestors needed to be aware that a tiger might be waiting to pounce. Most of us don't live with a tiger prowling our doorstep, but that sense

> **'When you are about to die, is it true that your life passes before your eyes?' asked the student.**
>
> **'Yes,' replied the monk. 'But God inserts a laugh track.'**
>
> Thai proverb

of vigilance is still ticking away in the background. And because our brain is designed to focus on possible threats which might kill us, when we are angry or upset with somebody, or are harbouring resentment, our brain brings us back to that thought and our body produces stress hormones.'

But actively choosing to take a positive approach can turn things on their head, Noel says: 'How do you want to feel – happy or stressed? If you tell yourself to think nice things about somebody, they stop being a threat inside your brain and you feel better about them and the whole situation. Being mindful about what you nurture in your own mind is one of the greatest tools for wellbeing that there is.'

Finally, 'Be more childlike,' Noel urges. 'Kids are programmed to seek stimulation as it promotes neurological growth, so are generally happy-go-lucky.'

Sanuk on the move – Jackie Winitkun and the Magic of Thailand

Every summer, a very sanuk festival travels across the UK. A mini Thailand is created in British cities for two fun-filled days.

It's the brainchild of Jackie Winitkun who, feeling homesick for her home country, put on an event in Poole to bring the experience of Thailand to her adopted home. 'I knew that getting together to eat food and enjoy sanuk would be a big attraction for Thais and Western people, too,' she says. And the 2012 show proved so popular that now the Magic of Thailand spreads sanuk in 10 cities for tens of thousands of festivalgoers.

The festival is a snapshot of Thailand, no plane ticket required. Fifty-plus stallholders showcase the best of Thai food and crafts and culture, with traditional dancing, massage, blessings from Thai monks, a Muay Thai boxing ring, a ladyboy show and an eating challenge. The Brighton show is a summer highlight; Sit, Siam and I go every year, loving the chance to meet up with friends and eat ourselves into a food coma.

For Jackie, sanuk is looking for the good and the fun in whatever situation you're in: 'There's always a way of finding fun,' she says. 'If something goes wrong, you can make it sanuk. Don't focus on the bad that happened; instead, think about what went well. What's the new way to have fun in the situation you now find yourself in? There is a choice of how you feel about certain things, and we choose to feel happy.'

Sanuk in a nutshell!

The power of play

One of the ways we can inject the carefree fun of childhood into our lives is through play, and someone who has made a career out of demonstrating how our personal wellbeing can be enriched by this is Yesim Kunter. After starting out as a toy designer, she now works with international brands running workshops to encourage innovation and creativity. 'As the philosopher Bertrand Russell said, "We don't stop playing because we grow older, we grow older because we stop playing,"' she says. 'Playfulness for any living thing is key for survival. If you can find small humour every day in your life it will make you feel lighter and be easier to connect to yourself.'

The play workshops Yesim runs help companies open divergent thinking among their employees and enable them to look at things from different perspectives. But we don't need to sign up for a training course; play is something we can all incorporate into our lives in whatever way we choose.

'Give yourself permission to do something out of the ordinary, something crazy,' recommends Yesim. 'Random situations are good. Things don't have to be perfect. For example, I go cold-water swimming all year round in the River Thames. There is a group of us and when we're doing the swim, we become totally engaged with life all around us. It can be 6am in the winter, the water is black, what is enjoyable? It's a crazy thing to do. But this is the adventure I get for my day. It only lasts five minutes – the river is 5°C! – but that risk taking, putting myself out of my comfort zone, is like being a child again. It's making the most of the moment and all about the joy.'

Now, even though I currently live on the English coast, I barely paddle in the chilly Channel, let alone swim (give me the tropical waters of the Gulf of Thailand any time). But enough of my friends have

Are You Having Fun?

embraced cold-water swimming for me to know that the buzz is addictive. Equally important is the camaraderie of doing it with a group of like-minded people. It's too potentially dangerous to be a solo activity, so involves sharing the experience with others – the perfect sanuk activity for hardy souls. As Yesim says, 'The aim is to all be together and enjoy the moment.'

Clinical psychologist Dr Jessamy Hibberd also recommends fun as an instant stress reliever, saying, 'Natural highs are the things that make you feel alive – anything that makes you feel good and doesn't have any negative after-effects. It can be your favourite music turned up loud, cooking an amazing meal, exercise, doing well at work, a great meeting, putting on a performance, relationships, kindness, giving back or being part of something bigger than you. Another great source of natural highs are our relationships – family, work and friends.'

For her book, *The Power of Fun: How to Feel Alive Again*, science journalist Catherine Price asked thousands of people around the world to describe their most fun and enjoyable experiences. The common thread she found was 'a magical blend of playfulness, connection, and flow'. The state of consciousness known as 'flow' was something the psychologist Mihaly Csikszentmihalyi was one of the first to identify and research. He discovered that people find genuine satisfaction when they are completely absorbed in an activity, especially one which involves their creative abilities. Studies have also found that fun is more fun when others are involved.

The beauty of sanuk is that it ticks all these boxes. It's within the reach of all of us and doesn't involve making a huge life transformation. In fact, small steps can lead to the greatest changes.

> 'What we do every day is what makes the biggest difference,' says Jessamy Hibberd. 'The choices we make every day shape our lives, little by little, step by step. Sometimes we trick ourselves that there's going to be some big answer that means everything will be great, but it doesn't need to be complicated. It can just be the simple stuff; engaging in your day-to-day life, appreciating what you have, empty time, connection, time for the things you enjoy. It's in reach for everyone. How we feel is a natural product of all our choices, but especially the small choices that each of us makes every day. And these small changes, when put together one by one can have a massive impact.'

As someone who used to be a sucker for a self-help book, over the years I've set countless goals, created spreadsheets, chanted positive mantras, cleared my clutter and reorganised my closets. While all had varying degrees of success, none turned out to be sustainable in the long term, which is why this simple philosophy of finding joy in the everyday resonates so much with me. What could be easier and more appealing than that?

SANUK TIP
Smile and say
something positive
every time you walk into
a room and notice the
reaction you get.

Sabai – sanuk's chilled-out cousin

Sanuk is all about bringing fun and pleasure into everyday life, but there are some other complementary concepts that also help explain why Thais are so happy. One of these is 'sabai', which means relaxed or comfortable. (Also: happy, feeling fine, content, healthy … you get the idea.) The concept of sanuk is closely linked to that of sabai, as keeping things relaxed is important for happiness. In fact, sabai sums up the Thai attitude to most things and has many uses. Here are just a few examples:

SABAI DEE MAI? – How are you? A common greeting; is everything well and good?

SABAI DEE – Well and good; the standard reply.

MAI SABAI – Not sabai; can be used for mood or health.

SABAI SABAI – Depending on the context, can mean everything is just great and couldn't be better; also used to describe a relaxing environment, and as an instruction to relax or take it easy. (The 80s' ballad 'Sabai Sabai' by Bird Thongchai is a Thai karaoke classic.)

SABAI JAI – At ease, content; literally, well heart.

NANG SABAI – Sit back and relax (nang means to sit).

The power of smiling

As nicknames go, the Land of Smiles is genius. I mean, who wouldn't want to visit there? And it perfectly sums up a nation full of the spirit of sanuk.

One of the things I immediately noticed when I first arrived in Thailand at the start of my big adventure was the sheer warmth and friendliness of everyone I met. Children, shopkeepers, train guards, shop workers … everywhere I went I was greeted with a smile. Coming from London, where grinning strangers are in short supply (or to be avoided if coming towards you on a dark night), this onslaught of good vibes took some getting used to.

> **Smile and the world smiles with you.**
>
> Stanley Gordon West

Admittedly, I was on an extended holiday, so already in high spirits, but being around so much cheerfulness made it hard to be in a bad mood. Now science confirms what seems obvious – being surrounded by smiling faces has tangible benefits.

When we're having fun, we naturally smile, which encourages the release of serotonin, a neurotransmitter which contributes to our happiness and wellbeing, as well as boosting the immune system.

We all know that when we see someone smiling, we smile back. And that's not just a social reflex; smiling turns out to be as contagious as yawning. It's so potent, we may be able to catch one from ourselves by smiling at ourselves in the mirror. Even forcing a fake smile can trick your brain into believing you're happy which can then spur actual feelings of happiness.

And of course, there's nothing more international than a smile; it's a way to communicate when you don't have the words.

The 13 types of smile

The Thai smile isn't just a reflection of their positive and fun-loving approach to life; smiling is deeply ingrained in their culture as a gesture of politeness, respect and friendliness. It's a way to communicate goodwill, defuse tension and maintain a peaceful atmosphere. In fact, Thais smile for so many reasons that, like the Inuits and their 50 words for snow, some observers have described 13 different types of yim – smile.

YIM TANG NAM TA – Translated as 'smiling with tears in my eyes', basically, I'm so happy I could cry.

YIM TUK TAI – The 'greeting smile', a polite smile of acknowledgment to someone you don't know, such as a neighbour you happen to pass in the street.

YIM CHEUM CHOM – The 'admiring smile'. Imagine a proud parent watching their offspring in a school concert.

FUEN YIM – A stiff smile which hides your true feelings.

YIM MEE LEDNAI – The sly smile used when covering up something.

YIM YAW – A teasing grin, or a mocking smirk which may be hiding secret knowledge.

YIM YOH YAE – The forced smile of someone feeling shy or embarrassed.

YIM HAENG – The 'dry smile' used in an awkward situation, such as confessing to being unable to repay a debt.

YIM SAO – The 'sad smile', when you know things aren't going to work out the way you'd hoped.

YIM THAK THAN – Used to politely disagree with someone; essentially, I understand but don't want to do it.

YIM CHEUA CHUAN – Flashed by winners to losers, this signifies having the upper hand.

YIM SOO – Smiling in the face of hardship; you haven't given up hope despite the odds.

YIM MAI AWK – You're trying to smile but it's just impossible (perhaps the results don't go your way on election night).

Want to see how this might work in practice? (Of course you do!) Check out the video created by English-language news site The Thaiger on their You Tube channel.

The Little Book of Sanuk

Choose happy

The best news of all is that every one of us can take steps to maintain or boost how happy we feel. In fact, the charity Action for Happiness, which works to help people learn practical, evidence-based ways to increase their wellbeing, say that while lots of factors impact how happy we feel, science shows that our conscious choices can make a difference. We can all learn skills that help us to feel happier.

Their Head of Psychology and Workplaces, Vanessa King, has crunched all the scientific research on what really works and come up with 10 Keys to Happier Living. 'We all want to lead a happy life but as a society we're not giving the things that science shows matter most enough priority,' she says. 'The good news is that our actions and choices can affect our happiness. Once our basic needs are met, what really is most likely to make us happy has less to do with our money and possessions and more to do with our attitudes, actions and relationships with other people.'

Their 10 Keys to Happier Living make fascinating reading and dovetail so closely with the concept of sanuk that I wanted to share them here:

1. Giving: do things for others. Helping other people is not only good for them, but for us, too. Giving also creates stronger connections between people and helps build a happier society for everyone.

2. Relating: connect with people. Our close relationships with family and friends provide love, meaning, support and increase our feelings of self-worth, while our broader social networks bring a sense of belonging.

3. Exercising: take care of your body. Our bodies and minds are connected. Being active makes us happier, improves our moods and can even lift us out of depression.

4. Awareness: notice the world around you. Learning to be more mindful and aware gets us in tune with our feelings and stops us dwelling on the past or worrying about the future, so we get more out of the day to day.

5. Trying out: keep learning new things. Learning exposes us to new ideas and helps us stay curious and engaged. It gives us a sense of accomplishment and boosts our self-confidence.

6. Direction: have goals to look forward to. Feeling good about the future is important for our happiness. Choosing meaningful but realistic goals gives our lives direction and brings a feeling of achievement when we succeed.

7. Resilience: find ways to move forward from difficulties. We often can't choose what happens to us, but we can choose how we react. It's not always easy, but one of the exciting findings from recent research is that resilience can be learned.

8. Emotions: take a positive approach. Although we need to be realistic about life's ups and downs, it helps to focus on the good aspects of any situation.

9. Acceptance: become comfortable with who you are. Being kinder to yourself when things go wrong increases your enjoyment of life and helps you to accept others as they are. See your mistakes as opportunities to learn and notice things you do well, however small.

10. Meaning: people who have meaning and purpose in life are happier, feel more in control and get more out of what they do. It can come from anything that involves being connected to something bigger than ourselves.

There's an oft-quoted statistic which claims that children smile about 400 times a day, yet adults only manage 20. I've not been able to track down the research behind this, but even if it's not a definitive number, the proven benefits of living a more fun-filled life are within the grasp of all of us, and in the following chapters I'll show how sanuk helps us to make the most out of every day, one smile at a time.

2.

Time to Reconnect

– Chuam Tor Ka Phu Khun

If you've ever felt there must be more to life, there is, and it's right here in front of us – we just need to stop and take notice.

Action for Wellbeing

It's a scene that plays out in bars across the country every night of the week: a group of people gathered around a table, drinks in front of them, dressed to kill – but all with their heads down, staring at their individual screens. Or the date-night couple sitting opposite one another in a restaurant, both looking at their phones, not at one another …

Smartphones, laptops and tablets have transformed our lives, but there's no denying that the digital age has sapped the spirit of sanuk from our social interactions. In today's modern world, we're together but apart; we've never been more connected, yet felt so alone.

Worryingly, technology is alienating us from one another and creating an environment which is the antithesis of sanuk. All the latest research shows that true happiness lies in rewarding relationships, that human connection is crucial and that the happiest and healthiest people are those who have warm connections with others.

And while we may have hundreds of 'friends' online, people's in-person networks have, in fact, shrunk over the last 35 years. Data overload is a major cause of why we don't spend as much time interacting in person with friends, family and work colleagues.

Social media, rather than making us feel genuinely connected, contributes to loneliness and reduces overall life satisfaction. In fact, one study found that the more hours people – particularly children – spent on Facebook, the less happy they felt over time. Much of this is because the curated versions of ourselves that we all present to the world don't always reflect our actual lives: those perfect images of our kids (taken just before one of them threw up over your expensive new top) ... the 'checking in' at the airport en route to an exotic holiday (with no mention of the blazing row in the car on the way) … the brilliant new job offer (that you're quietly terrified about) … the amazing partner who found the perfect birthday present (damn, you were thinking about ending the relationship) … We think we know what people's lives are like from their online profiles, and spending our spare time scrolling through idealised versions of our friends' lives leaves us feeling less attractive, less secure about our careers and generally unhappier with our own lives.

The trap of 'fake fun'

Science journalist and author Catherine Price coined the term 'fake fun' for activities that take up our leisure time but don't bring any meaningful joy. She describes it as 'essentially the junk food of our leisure time'. Now, I'm not claiming that no Thai person has ever wasted an evening scrolling through Netflix looking for something to watch, but with social connection at the heart of their culture, they will generally choose true fun with one another over 'fake'.

In Thailand, there's a phrase which encapsulates the intent behind this: 'pid mode online cheum huajai kab kon bon lok jing', which translates as, 'shut down online mode, and connect your heart with real people'.

Of course, it's not easy. As tech has become more interlinked with our lives it's made itself indispensable. We rely on our phones to wake us in the morning, tell us the weather, show us how to get from A to B, do our weekly shop, buy travel tickets, browse romantic partners … Frankly, it's impossible to imagine life without them. But we need to be more mindful about their use.

Time is precious – Lee Hawker
and The Cabin Rehab

Lee Hawker is someone who knows all about addiction. As clinical director at The Cabin Rehab, an addiction rehabilitation centre in Khua Mung, Thailand, he has helped successfully treat thousands of people suffering from substance abuse, alcohol addiction and gambling dependence.

Lee says that the hold our digital devices have over us is so powerful that it can be on a par with those of drugs and drink. As patients enter rehab, Lee sees this in action: 'The biggest argument we have with inpatients at our clinic is not to do with drugs or alcohol, but "Why do I have to hand my phone in?" They will fight to hold on to their phone.'

While the treatment centre doesn't ban phones completely, it does limit people's use in a bid to foster a sense of community and focus in on the real world, something Lee encourages us all to do.

'Technology can be wonderful, but time is precious, and the cost is breakdown of intimate relationships or broader family. Phones are things you own, which can come to own you. People talk more about what they've seen on Facebook and TikTok than real life; it's like you've lived your life watching TV and that's all you want to talk about. It's not possible to have a digital detox in today's interconnected world, but we can, and should, put some moderate restrictions of phone usage in place.'

It's a worrying trend which could lead to a cultural erosion, warns Lee. 'Sanuk is the bedrock of Thai culture, but that's changing for the younger Thai generation. This is a big shift from traditional values.

'Sanuk is all about the cultural value of extended family and being in the moment, but Thailand is like everywhere in the world – moving at a faster pace and losing something in the process. Nearly all young people are constantly looking at their phones – in the restaurants, at the mall. The young generation is about getting "likes", or some notification back, but they don't fully understand the paradox of getting validation and feedback from people they'll never meet. They're missing that of those closest to them.

'There was a time when we'd share intimate details of ourselves with our partner or family. Now younger people do it online. This has led to a breakdown of intimacy with friends and partners that makes them vulnerable.'

We can't turn the clock back on technology, but by strengthening social and family bonds and forming meaningful natural connections we can bring ourselves and others back from the virtual to the real world and create the opportunity for a more sanuk-filled life.

Under pressure

'Being in touch with people 24/7 means that there's a constant pressure on you,' says clinical psychologist Dr Jessamy Hibberd. 'When you're checking, updating or replying you're "on", and being in this state constantly is exhausting. When it's more severe it can also be a form of avoidance, as it's so absorbing it allows you to ignore the other stuff going on in your life.'

It's not just that the dopamine hit of a message alert is addictive; the increased stress that comes with the pressure to respond to messages at all times is bad for our wellbeing. If we don't give an instant response, we feel like we've failed.

Despite the cliché of teenagers glued to their phones, it's not just young people who are in the thrall of technology. Different age groups have different issues: for young people, it's social media; for their parents' generation, it can be linked to work and anxiety-based.

In my day job as a magazine director, I used to get at least 200 emails a day. Less than 5 per cent of these were ever relevant or useful, yet I still found myself clicking on them, just in case, then getting a buzz when I hit delete … it was a pointless activity, but strangely satisfying. It somehow made me feel like I was being productive.

According to Lee Hawker, this sounds symptomatic of something called high-functioning anxiety, which can be seen in some professionals. 'People have a fear of failure and anxiety,' he says. 'When you were growing up, letters were typed and posted. Now time is speeding up; deadlines are faster and shorter. Addiction is about getting a reward. Getting a notification of your next task, achieving it and ticking it off gives that dopamine rush. The cost is that we can't do that for long periods of time.'

After talking to Lee, I put aside an hour to locate and unsubscribe from the numerous mailing lists my details had made their way on to, and marked the senders to go to my Junk folder. Now my in-box feels less chaotic, and my head clearer. It's a feeling that's stayed with me over the months that have followed, too. Although that instant rush of dopamine might be mistaken for a feeling of sanuk, it's not. Instead, by replacing mindless distractions with meaningful connections we can create true and lasting sanuk.

Why multitasking doesn't work

After years of seeing my son Siam and his mates scrolling through social media on their phones, while watching a football match on someone's laptop, glancing up at *The Simpsons* on TV and eating their dinner, it's no surprise to read that young people are the age group most likely to be multitasking on their devices. Even 10 years ago, a poll by Ofcom found that those aged 16–24 are likely to do more than one task at a time, squeezing 14 hours and 7 minutes of media activity into each day, in just over 9 hours.

This lack of focus and not being in the moment is not just the opposite of sanuk, it could come with dangerous side effects, according to Dr Aric Sigman, a psychologist with an interest in child health. He told the BBC that prolonged screen time is a health and development issue for young people, with some of the adverse effects associated with it including obesity and diabetes. 'We need to think of recreational screen time as a form of consumption in the way that we think of sugar, fat, alcohol, hours in the sun – measured in units of hours per day.'

Worryingly, research is showing that multitasking is particularly damaging and could actually be altering our brains. They are built to focus, and when we try to concentrate on more than one task at a time we cause an overload of their processing capacity.

Dave Crenshaw, author of the book *The Myth of Multitasking*, explains that when we think we are multitasking, our brain is actually switching rapidly between the tasks. The constant effort this requires means that doing even just two or three things at once puts far more demand on our brains compared with doing them one after another.

Multitasking has been shown to have a negative physical effect, prompting the release of stress hormones and adrenaline. This can trigger a vicious cycle, whereby we work hard at multitasking, take longer to get things done, then feel stressed, harried and compelled to multitask more.

Dave's advice is to remove the 'busy' tag from your sense of self. Being busy does not make you valuable; it's what you do with the time that really matters. It's those relationships – the beating heart of sanuk – that are key. So when you're next tempted to glance down at your phone to check messages while in a meeting or out with friends, remind yourself how important it is to simply give people your full attention. Not to mention good manners.

What worked for me was the realisation that the more I multitasked, the more mistakes I made. Rather than saving time, it was having the opposite outcome as I had to go back to try to fix them. Awareness is all. Regaining your focus requires you to be mindful of how you – and others – are using technology.

Positive effects of tech

Of course, it's not all bad. Technology can be incredibly useful and educational, providing us with the tools for creativity, connectivity and fun. And while in-person experience almost always trumps digital, social media can undoubtedly give a warm feeling of belonging; the dopamine hit I get from those once-a-year birthday messages from old friends far and wide on my otherwise-dormant Facebook account will always spark joy – a small moment of sanuk.

In fact, some research shows that if we use social media actively to connect with each other, that's more likely to enhance wellbeing. It's the passive consumption that often lowers our wellbeing.

So by being more conscious about our use, we may be able to increase feelings of screentime sanuk. There's no 'ideal' amount of screentime. Content and context matter.

Psychotherapist Noel McDermott can see the positives. 'It's not as simplistic as online bad vs real-world good. Our lives are online now, and we won't be going back on that. Different generations use technology in different ways. For younger people, it's more complementary; they tend to initiate contact online then follow up in person. They integrate it much better than older generations.

'If we hadn't been online, the pandemic would have been much, much worse. We've seen the advantages of having the digital world at our fingertips with video calls, the capacity to be economically productive from home working and staying in touch with each other.

'The real problem for psychological growth is the algorithms which match you with people and content they think you might like. This stifles those diverse voices and opinions which are so crucial.'

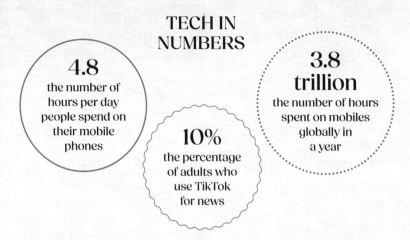

TECH IN NUMBERS

4.8
the number of
hours per day
people spend on
their mobile
phones

10%
the percentage
of adults who
use TikTok
for news

**3.8
trillion**
the number of hours
spent on mobiles
globally in
a year

How to bring some sanuk to your digital life

With so much of modern life lived online, tech isn't going anywhere
any time soon, but we can use the principles of sanuk to help stop it
ruling our lives – to communicate with people in person, ensure we
relate to each other in a meaningful way and to be more authentically
connected and happy. Here are some proven ways to free yourself
from the negative effects of tech without having to consign your
phone to the bin.

Try mindfulness

Practising mindfulness is a great way to switch off from the constant
hubbub of technology. It's about being completely aware of what's
happening in the present – of all that's going on inside and also that
around you. Take 10 minutes out of your day to switch off everything
and close your eyes. Concentrate on your breathing, how your body

SANUK TIP
Unfollow those people whose posts always make you feel inadequate. Be aware of what you consume: it's not called doomscrolling for nothing!

feels as you inhale in through the nose and out through the mouth. Once done, note how you feel, both in body and mind.

Do nothing

Sanuk is all about being in – and enjoying – the moment. And in today's hectic world we sometimes need to stop what we're doing to remind ourselves how to do that. Clinical psychologist, Dr Jessamy Hibberd recommends the power of empty time to just think. 'We used to let our minds wander without constantly being engaged,' she says. 'Empty time isn't wasted time; it's important to step back, switch off and reflect on where you are and where you're heading. It gives your mind a chance to wander and come up with new ideas. It allows you to check in with how you're feeling and to listen to your body and mind.' Downtime is an opportunity for the brain to make sense of what it has recently learned: 'It's like a mini version of when you go on holiday and come back with renewed motivation and everything feeling back under control. It's only by stopping that you can restart with a fresh sense of perspective.' Thai people prize relaxation and time spent hanging out with friends and family with no particular plans or schedule.

Cut it down, don't cut it out

While all the latest research shows that we need to be more be mindful of the time we spend on our devices, it may require less effort than we think. Even cutting your smartphone use by just one hour a day makes you less anxious, more satisfied with life and more likely to exercise, a study found in 2023. Researchers said it was 'not necessary to completely give up the smartphone to feel better', but they discovered that reducing its daily use had positive effects on a person's wellbeing. You can increase your chances of enjoying sanuk by making just a few simple lifestyle tweaks.

Try 'do not disturb'

Sleepless nights are sanuk-sappers, so limit tech to aid rest. If you want to drop off quicker, sleep more soundly and even improve your memory, it's worth turning on your phone's do-not-disturb function an hour before you go to bed: one 2020 study found that restricting mobile-phone use before bedtime for four weeks brought all these benefits. It's not just the danger of getting caught up for hours mindlessly scrolling and watching videos of golden retrievers/make-up contouring tutorials/(insert your own personal online rabbit holes here) – research shows that looking at your phone just before bed disrupts your sleep. That's because the blue light emitted by your screen inhibits the production of melatonin, the hormone that helps regulate your sleep cycle (the higher it is, the more likely you are to have a good night's rest).

Do something wild

Getting outdoors is one of the best ways to switch off from tech and tune into the world around you. And you'll feel better, too. Nature can provide strong feelings of sanuk. There are plenty of studies showing that being in green spaces can help to reduce stress and anxiety. One of my favourite UK charities is The Wildlife Trusts. It's a grassroots movement of people from all walks of life who believe that we need nature and nature needs us. Every year, since 2015, they have been doing something special. They set a challenge called 30 Days Wild which encourages everyone to enjoy nature in their neighbourhoods every day in June through daily Random Acts of Wildness. This could be something as simple as listening to birdsong, gazing at butterflies or making the most of local parks, gardens and school grounds. Over 3.5 million people have taken part, and there's now evidence to show that

it can make participants happier and healthier, particularly those who usually spent less time outdoors.

The impact of taking part in 30 Days Wild has been tracked by academics at the University of Derby. Their study found that people who did something 'wild' each day for a month, felt happier, healthier and more connected to nature, says Dr Miles Richardson, director of psychology at the university: 'Two months after completing the challenge all those taking part benefitted, feeling 30 per cent healthier than when they started. They had a sustained increase in happiness, health, connection to nature and pro-nature behaviours, such as feeding birds and planting flowers for bees – not just during the challenge, but for months afterwards. Truly engaging with nature and appreciating its beauty is key to the life satisfaction the natural world can bring.'

11 ways to press pause

1.
Put your phone/tablet/ laptop in another room, so you must consciously go and get it.

2.
Turn off your updates.

3.
Get out of the habit of immediately replying to people.

4.
Make a rule not to have phones at the table during mealtimes.

5.
Read a book.

6.
Keep your phone in your bag when you go out – or even leave it at home.

7.
Move your phone out of the bedroom.

8.
Take a social media vacation; try having a day off with no posts or updates.

9.
Let yourself get bored occasionally; that's when some of the best ideas come.

10.
Restrict social media use, setting a daily time limit.

11.
Try a morning without the phone.

3.

Family, Friends, Loved Ones

– Khun Ti Khun Rak

To love is nothing.
To be loved is
something.
But to love and be
loved is everything.

Thai proverb

Family, friends and social ties are at the heart of Thai life. These relationships are the bedrock of sanuk in Thailand, and strengthening those bonds is key to feelings of happiness and wellbeing. It's not so easy to be sanuk if you're alone; being around others in social harmony is what makes an experience sanuk, and Thai people instinctively know what all the latest research is showing – that good relationships are more important than money and success for happiness.

As a collective, rather than individualistic society, embedded in the Thai DNA is the understanding that relationships don't just make us happy, they also help us to weather the unhappy times. Western studies are now bringing the importance of these relationships into sharp focus – and one man is spearheading the research: Dr Robert Waldinger. As a professor of psychiatry at Harvard Medical School and director of the Harvard Study of Adult Development at Massachusetts General Hospital (the world's longest happiness study, which has been running since 1938) he knows a thing or two about how we can all be happier.

His TED talk 'What Makes a Good Life?' has racked up nearly 44 million views and is one of the most watched ever. Dr Waldinger has examined what really makes us thrive and found that the breadth and depth of our relationships are keys to wellbeing – not just happiness, but physical health, too. He has boiled down the definition of a good life to this sanuk statement: 'Being engaged in activities I care about with people I care about'.

Dr Waldinger's conclusion is that human connection is our superpower, saying, 'The surprising finding is that our relationships and how happy we are in our relationships has a powerful influence on our health. The Harvard study reveals that the strength of our connections with others can predict the health of both our bodies and our brains as we go through life. Good relationships help us get through life's inevitable challenges. Taking care of your body is important, but tending to your relationships is a form of self-care too.'

With close relationships acting as better predictors of long and happy lives than money, social class, IQ or even genes, the benefits of forming close ties and living a sanuk-filled life have never been clearer.

Family – Krob Krua

Thais welcome any excuse to have a party. Every time we land in Thailand, even after just a few months' absence, three generations of our extended family will be gathered waiting for us in the arrivals hall at Bangkok's Suvarnabhumi Airport. They'll drape flower garlands around our necks in greeting, then we'll pile into the minibus they've hired for the occasion, and the sanuk will start as we inch our way through gridlocked city traffic to home, where a feast will be waiting.

Family comes first in Thailand with a great emphasis placed on the extended family. The older generation are treated in high regard. Looking after loved ones is expected, with those who can afford it helping others without expecting to be repaid. With a culture of respect for seniors and taking care of parents, it's accepted that you'll look after your elders, like they did for you when you were young. It's just repaying the favour.

> **Family is not an important thing. It's everything.**
>
> Thai proverb

Thai family dictionary

Grandparents on each side of the family are called by a different name, while yai can be used as a generic term for older women:

MAA – Mum

PHAW – Dad

PU – Father's father

TAA – Mother's father

YAA – Father's mother

YAI – Mother's mother (also used for elderly women, to show respect)

Everyone together

Traditional Thai living is sanuk society in action; with connection, community and belonging at its heart. Family interdependency is common and several generations may live in the same house, with everyone helping out. This is done willingly and uncomplainingly, and always in the spirit of sanuk. As well as being a way of countering the cost of childcare, youngsters thrive. A study by United for All Ages (UAA) shows that children who mix with older people feel secure and loved and have better reading and social skills, while a strong and positive family-support system from a young age leads to better mental health in adulthood.

There are health and societal benefits at the older end of the age spectrum, too. According to the Institute for Fiscal Studies, increased social contact between the ages of 50 and 70 is associated with a lower risk of developing dementia. Age is also an important marker of one's place in the community and pervades every aspect of daily life in Thai culture. While Thai society is set up that way, with no real system of care homes, families are happy to pull together to look after their elderly members.

As Thai children grow older, there's no rush for them to leave home. As a typical Western teenager in the 1980s, I was out of the door at 18, with barely a backward glance; it felt like a crucial step towards becoming an independent adult. In Thailand, however, young people may stay with their parents until they get married, though more modern-day young Thais do now move out but still live very close to their parents.

Every family is different, but healthy families are the building blocks of a healthy society, and the blend of generations has the capacity to lead to a happier, more sanuk way of living. Even just being together as a family increases daily wellbeing, while sharing experiences with loved ones is a wonderful way to create lasting memories and strengthen your relationships.

A different way of living

We can use the Thai approach as inspiration to create healthier, more sanuk-filled societies all over the world. In a trend accelerated by the cost-of-living crisis, older adults are moving back in with their parents, grandparents are moving in with their kids and grandkids, and 20–30-somethings often have no choice but to stay put in their childhood homes due to lack of funds. During the pandemic, which forced so many of us apart, some families moved in together to provide support. Of course, this comes with its challenges. 'What on earth is sanuk about moving back in with our parents or in-laws?' I hear my British friends wearily sigh. And I get it. Leaving home is a sign of coming of age, so returning can seem like a backward step. But perhaps it's time to look to Thai culture and start thinking about different ways of living. Consider this: 1.8 million UK households contain two or more adult generations – up 38 per cent in a decade; and if this trend continues, it's expected to triple by 2040.

Is multi-generational living for you?

Sanuk wins

- Mortgage, bills and food costs are split, leaving more money for fun stuff.
- Cheaper date nights for couples with kids.
- A chance to get closer as a family.
- You'll never be lonely.
- Communal living and cooking together can be full of sanuk potential.

Sanuk spoilers

- It will take planning, effort and sacrifice.
- Lack of privacy – and tense queues for the bathroom.
- Danger of reverting back to childhood dynamics.
- Young kids can be noisy and exhausting for older relatives.
- Differing parenting styles can cause arguments.

Four ways to inter-gen harmony

1.

Remember why you're doing it.
Grounding yourself in the big picture
will stop you getting frustrated when
something – or someone – annoys you.

2.

Get privacy laws in place.
Everyone needs a space they can
retreat to, however small.

3.

Set boundaries.
What are the expectations – from who's
paying for groceries to parenting styles?

4.

Communicate.
Call a family meeting to nip things
in the bud before they escalate.

An alternative option to moving in together is moving closer to each other. Two of my new-mum friends are about to leave London to be nearer their parents, triggered by childcare fees which are more than their salaries. (However much you enjoy your job, working at a loss is very much not sanuk.) They're fortunate to have good relationships with their folks, so doting grandparents close by to babysit is an obvious draw.

If moving is just too impractical or unappealing, put regular check-ins in place. Video calls are better than phone calls for reducing feelings of loneliness, and setting up a regular time for a family chat is one of the best ways to ensure you can catch up and be uninterrupted. Or go old school and write a letter. Who doesn't love a beautiful handwritten envelope dropping through the door? Include photos to add to the sanuk feeling.

The importance of family support and care of the elderly is deeply ingrained in Thai culture, but, ultimately, it comes down to a sense of gratitude and appreciation. At a time when ageing is increasingly an industry of outsourced care, with the stress and cost of care homes which come with it, there is much to be learned from Thai culture about what makes a good life in old age and how we should treat the elderly.

If you have a difficult relationship with your family, try to focus on the qualities that your parents do have. Find support and solidarity with siblings. Finally, if all else fails, practise acceptance: the best way to deal with parents who can't be your friends is to accept this fact for what it is.

Friends – Peuan

Not everyone is lucky enough to have close family ties, but we can all forge the same kind of relationships with friends. Having strong friendships is critical to our wellbeing, too; one study has shown that loneliness is as bad for people's health as smoking 15 cigarettes per day. In fact, there's a lot of research showing that the benefits of spending sanuk time with friends can go far beyond the moment itself. As well as helping us feel more balanced and connected, our friends help us get things in perspective and manage life's problems. We need close platonic relationships, and they can affect everything from how long we live to how susceptible we are to mental-health issues. A strong social circle brings with it a host of benefits; and the proven advantages of finding like-minded people to hang out with makes friendship worth the effort.

> **Friends for a meal are easy to find; friends until end of life are difficult to find.**
>
> Thai proverb

Making friends as an adult

If you're experiencing a friendship recession, don't worry too much – it's probably not personal. Friends can come and go as we pass through different life stages. Usually, it's more to do with drifting apart than any dramatic falling out; connections fade, people and our relationships with them change and we have less in common than we once did. The pals we once partied with start to settle down and have kids, best friends move away, a work buddy gets a new job the other side of town … Whatever the reason, there's nothing to be gained by sitting at home bemoaning the fact that you have a smaller social circle than you once had. Friendship doesn't just happen organically – take responsibility, rather than waiting passively.

Which friend are you?

PEUAN – Friend

PEUAN TEE DEE TEE SOOD – Best friend

PEUAN SA NID – Close friend

PEUAN TDAI – Friend who would die for you

PEUAN TAE – True friend

PUEAN TEE SUASAT – Loyal friend

PEUAN RAAK – Love friend

Sanuk happens with others, and as our friends are one of the main ingredients to a life filled with fun, there's no better excuse for getting out and actively searching for a new crew who fit with who you are right now. Of course, that can be a daunting prospect. It's much easier to find a new Netflix series to fill your time with, but genuine sanuk is in short supply when we mindlessly binge-watch TV. Think about a memory that makes you smile, and it's probably not Season 5 of *Breaking Bad*; it's much more likely to be a time when you were sharing sanuk with friends.

This is where social media actually lives up to its name. From local Facebook groups to friendship apps, you can find like-minded people and events in your area which chime with your interests. You might not gain a new best friend, but finding people for different interests in your life, at different stages, is a way to bring sanuk into your life. Too shy or nervous? Don't be. It will go better than you think, according to an encouraging study which found people actually like you more than you think they do. The authors termed this the 'liking gap', whereby we're inclined to underestimate how interesting strangers think we are.

FRIENDSHIPS IN NUMBERS

Research by British anthropologist Robin Dunbar suggests the average person has:

3-5
very close
friends

10-15
friends in
their circle

100-150
acquaintances
in their social
network

Five steps to get to know new people

1.

Find your tribe: go online or check
neighbourhood noticeboards or shop windows.

2.

**Make a note of any local events
they're holding.**

3.

Get out of your comfort zone,
off your sofa and show up.

4.

**Say hello when you get there;
introduce yourself to other
people; get their phone numbers.**

5.

Follow up after the event and
ask them to hang out.

Creating a sense of sanuk in your friendships

Even if you're blessed with a wide circle of friends, being with them might not always feel sanuk. Our busy lives mean that friendships can suffer. You might love them dearly, but sometimes, getting a message from a friend wanting to meet up can trigger a sense of calendar-juggling weariness, rather than excitement, not to mention those WhatsApp group chats which never actually turn into a fun IRL experience. Busy schedules can mean that weeks turn into months, and when you do finally meet up, you all exclaim amazement that you've left it so long. If this sounds all-too familiar, it's time to give your friendships a bit of TLC.

Just like our romantic relationships, friendships can go stale as we start taking one another for granted. Quality time together matters. One guaranteed source of sanuk is to share experiences – whether that's swapping your usual gossipy coffee for a museum visit, a spa trip or playing at being a tourist in your own town; going somewhere different can spark new conversations, rather than rehashing your usual topics. Creating new memories is a great way to strengthen your friendship bonds.

But in the same way that relationships can sometimes run their course, so can friendships. If you get an active sense of dread at the thought of spending time with someone, despite trying everything to keep the sanuk spark alive, that's ok, too. Not all friendships are meant to be for life.

SANUK TIP

Friends are the family you choose – so choose to spend time with those people who lift you up, rather than bring you down.

Six friendship tips from the experts at Relate

1. Give and take may be a cliché, but equality matters. Strive for balance between who talks and who listens, who is the shoulder to cry on and who takes responsibility for initiating getting together.

2. **We may feel extra connected when we have things in common, but we learn most when we have differences, so try to embrace them as chances to stretch yourself and grow.**

3. There are no right and wrongs with friendships – some people have only one or two close friends, while others have a big group and some have different friends for different parts of their lives. Do what's right for you.

4. **Our time is precious, and we need to spend it with those who matter most to us. If you stay connected to someone out of guilt or because it's a habit, then maybe it's time to move on.**

5. Misunderstandings that are not resolved can fester and can even destroy friendships. If your friendship is valuable to you, face the issue and have a conversation, even if it's difficult or embarrassing, it's better than losing a friend.

6. **Friends can be a great support when times are tough but make sure you can follow through on what you promise. This might mean not being too ambitious with your offers – better to be realistic and able to do what you say.**

Loved ones – Khun Ti Khun Rak

On my last night in the UK before heading off on my big adventure back in the 1990s, I stayed on the sofa in the shared London flat where I used to live. I had an early flight, so had turned down the offer of going clubbing with my soon-to-be ex-flatmate in favour of getting some sleep. I was rudely awoken when she rocked up later that night with a rowdy gang of people in tow. On hearing I was flying to Asia in a few hours, one pulled something out of his jacket pocket. By some bizarre serendipity, he had just come back from his round-the-world travels and just so happened to have a map of the Thai island of Koh Pha Ngan on him. Grabbing a pen, he circled a beach and scribbled 'Bio's' on it. 'Great food, great vibe … you've got to go there.' It was too random a coincidence to turn down, so I tucked the map away in my backpack.

Arriving in Thailand months later, after adventures in India and Nepal, I dug out the crumpled paper, figuring that the drunken stranger's recommendation would be as good a place as any to start. Bio's turned out to be Bio's Dynamic Kitchen – a group of ramshackle bamboo huts and a chilled-out bar/restaurant where I was soon spending most of my time. That's where I met Sit, who was running the place while owner Bio was away. I spoke no Thai and his English was more than a bit hit and miss as he'd learned it by listening to rock lyrics, but we had a lot of fun getting to know one another. His sanuk approach to life, along with a constant supply of delicious dishes, helped win my heart and we fell in love.

I can guarantee that had I met Sit in my old London life, things would have gone very differently. In my metropolitan media existence, I was part of a world where everyone and everything was judged through a narrow (and in retrospect, limiting) lens of 'cool'. I didn't take the time to appreciate the value of those who weren't just like me and my friends. And while I certainly hadn't gone travelling looking for a husband, by taking a more relaxed, sanuk approach to life, I'd opened myself up to new relationship possibilities.

Navigate the modern dating scene

There's a lot of talk about how the fun has gone out of meeting a partner. Today's world of dating apps offers so many options it's easy to keep swiping in search of perfection. And if you do go on a date, every single moment must be picture perfect. But as discussed in Chapter 2, by stepping back from tech, looking up from our phones and connecting with those around us, we can bring a feeling of sanuk back to our lives – and that includes our love lives.

So go old school. Get off the dating apps and get out. Wherever you are, look around the room to see if anyone is looking at you. If they are, and you're interested, hold their gaze. Want to open up even more options? Why not throw a singles party and host a dinner for unattached friends and friends of friends. The intensity of a one-on-one date can be intimidating, but this way you get to meet a bunch of potential partners, and even if you don't hit it off romantically with anyone, you'll get to share a sanuk experience.

11 sanuk couple activities

1.

Share hobbies.
Doing things you
both enjoy creates
warm, shared
memories.

2.

Travel together.
Exploring new
places and having
adventures as a team
promotes bonding.

3.

Get physical.
Exercising or
playing sports
together helps you
stay active and
connected.

4.

Have a movie night.
Settle down with popcorn
and relax and bond in your
own home.

5.

Try a new recipe.
Cooking together can
be intimate, plus you
get to enjoy the food
afterwards.

The Little Book of Sanuk

6.

Take a dance class.
Learning some new moves
is a fun way to bring you
physically closer.

7.

Go to a wine tasting.
Knowing your Merlot from your
Malbec is an adult skill that will
make dinners out more sanuk, too.

8.

Take a trip down memory lane.
Scroll through the photos on your phones
and social media and even old prints – can
you find your first picture together?

9.

**Have a tech-free
date day.**
Go for a walk, or
simply stay home
with no distractions.

10.

Visit each other's hometowns.
Sharing stories from the past
is a great way to find out more
about your partner.

11.

Sing a karaoke duet.
Whether you can hold a
tune or not, it will be an
unforgettable moment of fun.

Thai love talk

Sanuk stems from true emotions, and Thai people speak from the heart when it comes to feelings:

JAI – Heart

DEE JAI – Good heart (happy)

SIA JAI – Lose heart (sad)

AO JAI – To please or behave well

JEP JAI – Feel hurt

SEE A JAI – Broken hearted

POOM JAI – Proud

JAI RAWN – Hot heart (quick temper)

JAI DEE – Good heart (kind)

SON JAI – To care or be interested

JAI LAI – Mean heart

CASE STUDY

Wooed with food – Potchara 'Prieo' To-uam, relationship counsellor

Prieo works with Counselling Thailand in Chiang Mai, Northern Thailand, and says it's no surprise that my holiday romance started when Sit wooed me with food: 'In Thailand, when someone asks, "What kind of food would you like to have?" it's a way to show they are interested in you and would like to please you.' With food playing a central role in sanuk good times (a topic we'll cover in Chapter 10), Thai people take every opportunity to meet and eat, so relationships are often formed over meals. As Prieo notes: 'Thai people love to celebrate something. In fact, growing up in the countryside, celebrations and family gatherings would be how we meet potential partners.'

Close family ties mean that parental approval is key, so when things start to get serious it's time for families to meet. 'Without that happening, things are much more complicated,' says Prieo. 'It's important to introduce both sides to each other, so they understand the culture of the family and understand their sense of sanuk. How they enjoy their sanuk might be different from yours.' In my case, food was once again a common ground. It helped to bridge the gap between different cultures. When I met Sit's family, they soon learned my favourite dishes and still make a point of serving them when I visit. In the UK, Sit connected with my parents by preparing legendary Thai feasts whenever we got together.

Nearly 30 years later, mealtimes for the two of us are still an important part of our sanuk, and while every couple can find their own way to strengthen their bond, Thai food on tap is a sanuk win for me.

Mix it up

We should be encouraging more mixing of generations for all, not just within family groups, says Stephen Burke, director of a 'think and do' tank and social enterprise called United for All Ages. Bringing people together is one of the biggest challenges in this new decade, he says. 'The last decade saw huge disconnection and division. The 2020s can be different. Promoting more intergenerational mixing could help create a nation for all ages by 2030 – united not divided.'

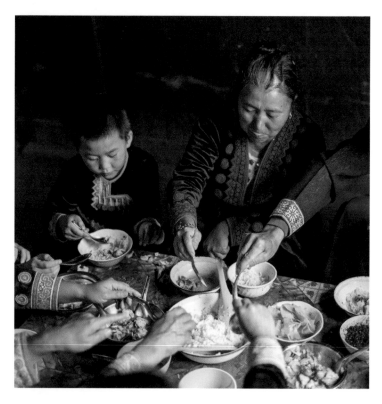

The group's report, 'Together in the 2020s', argues that intergenerational projects could help tackle social problems such as poor health, loneliness, ageism and housing. It warns that children and young people face a crisis of confidence, often fearful about the future. Their solution? Turning care homes into community hubs or linking them with nurseries, scaling up home-sharing schemes for older and younger people and redesigning the economy to make the most of the ageing society. 'More mixing between the generations is the way to build trust and understanding across our communities,' says Stephen. 'To make it happen requires not just vision and ambition, but also political will and leadership.'

This is also something we can all do in our everyday lives. If you have a skill or talent, offer to host a workshop on it at your local care home. This doesn't need to take up too much time and could make a huge difference to residents' wellbeing. It could be anything from a gentle chair-yoga class to a poetry-reading afternoon, an art-group session or passing on any digital skills you have.

And as sanuk is all about making connections, every member of the family can get involved. If you're a UK dog owner, and your four-legged friend has the right temperament, they could get involved, too. Pets As Therapy (see Resources, p. 265) dogs come in all shapes and sizes and can bring great comfort and joy to pet lovers who are no longer able to have a dog of their own.

The quest to reclaim lost sanuk

For Sit and me life was carefree and so sanuk that our holiday romance blossomed into marriage and parenthood … But fast forward a few years, and the reality of juggling work and family life on a different continent meant that fun sometimes seemed in short supply. In the UK, people spoke faster, were in more of a hurry and less inclined to make an effort with a foreigner. We needed to reclaim our lost sanuk, so we went back to the tropical island beach where we first met.

Our relationship reset may have been at the expensive end of the spectrum, but if you're struggling with your relationship, it's a smart idea to resurrect what you were doing when you fell in love – or come up with ideas for new things you will both enjoy. And if you've lost that loving feeling in your relationship, focus on bringing back a sense of joy. We're told so often that relationships are hard work, but we can work so hard that we forget to make time for hopes, dreams, play and just plain fun. Essentially, it's about remembering why you got together in the first place and regaining that sense of sanuk. The happiest couples are happy because they have a lot of fun together. It's so easy to let day-to-day life suck the sanuk out of a relationship, but what better reason could there be to prioritise pleasure?

> **Arguments are never won, only lost.**
>
> Thai proverb

Perhaps, if you do just one thing here, plan a novelty date night. New experiences activate the brain's reward system, flooding it with the same chemicals as those aroused when we're falling in love.

SANUK TIP

Make a gratitude list of all your partner's strengths, so that you remember why you first fell in love with them.

With Sit and Siam. Trips to the island where we met are always family sanuk

SANUK TIP
Schedule in some frivolous couple time involving new and exciting activities – this is consistently associated with better relationships.

5:1 – the magic ratio

After 50 years researching what makes for lasting love, American psychologist Dr John Gottman found that the difference between happy and unhappy couples is the balance between positive and negative interactions. Couples are happier if, for every one disagreement, misunderstanding or hurt feeling, there are five positive, affectionate, caring or fun interactions to counterbalance it. These don't just have to be obvious ones like expressing affection, but also laughing and teasing. Enjoying sanuk with one another is a powerful bonding tool.

Breaking up the sanuk way

If it's not just the fun that's gone out of a relationship, but the love, too, ensure that any break-up is mindful and has connections at its core. And that means doing it in person, rather than via text or worse, ghosting. Being sensitive to others' feelings is an important part of true sanuk. So while it's undoubtedly hard to look someone in the eye and tell them you don't love them anymore, by being kind and practising empathy you can ensure you get closure for you both.

Make sure you have emotional support from friends and family, too – a relationship breakdown is never easy, even if you are the one who instigates it. Let one or two of those closest to you know in advance, so they can be there to help you and give you love when you might feel lost and alone. Quality – and even sanuk – times with loved ones will help you feel connected.

4.

Community and Volunteering

– Chumchun Lae Asa
Samak

The more we
develop love
for others, the
more confidence
we will have in
ourselves.

Dalai Lama

It's easy to be social in Thailand. Warm evenings all year round mean Thai people often dine outdoors, with tables and chairs set up outside their homes. As they sit eating and chatting, they take the opportunity to catch up with any familiar – or not-so-familiar – faces passing by. When we came back to the UK, I realised how much time we spend behind closed doors, and how little contact I had with our neighbours. The solution came in the sanuk shape of Bella, our Golden Retriever puppy. Every time we left the house with her, we'd invariably find ourselves chatting, not just with other dog owners, but with everyone who crossed our path. Whatever the weather, our walks turned into a sanuk outing. Sadly, Bella passed away a few years ago, and one of the many reasons I miss her is the absence of those enjoyably random conversations. One of her lasting legacies, however, is that some of those strangers became good friends who I still spend time with today.

Although others we met are less present in my life, being connected to this kind of wider community matters. Whether it's casual acquaintances you bump into at the gym, the woman who catches the same train as you every morning, the barista in your local coffee shop, they're more crucial than anyone used to realise. There are a host of words to describe these kinds of people – peripheral friendships, consequential strangers, weak ties – but whatever you want to call them, they matter.

Gillian Sandstrom, Senior Lecturer in the Psychology of Kindness at the University of Sussex, has made a study of this, and says that while you don't necessarily have to know the other person's name, they need to be someone who is familiar to you from having seen them, or interacted with them previously.

Her research has found that these kinds of 'minimal interactions' give us a boost by helping us feel connected to people and giving a sense of belonging.

As well as increasing life satisfaction, having a broader cross section of people in our lives actually benefits our more intimate relationships too, as it can help prevent us being too reliant on those closest to us. By having a range of people to fill different needs it can take the pressure off a few.

While I'd never be so bold as to say that sanuk is a silver bullet that can heal our divided world, it can help us with the building blocks of connection. Today, we have a lack of ritual, community or shared meaning in our lives, but we can all increase our wellbeing by strengthening our ties with one another. For anyone who is not typically sociable or doesn't have large family networks, the same health benefits can be gained through volunteering and giving back to your community.

We can learn from Thai culture by creating this more neighbourly way of living. As a collectivistic society, rather than considering their individual needs and desires, they tend to lean into what's best for the community, their neighbours, as well as their family. The importance of social ties means that groups are more important than individuals.

The traditional Thai values of empathy and community feeling are key in promoting wellbeing and they help encourage sanuk for all. As humans, we need real-life emotional contact, and the more we have, the happier we are. In a sanuk twist, happiness spreads through social networks and turns out to be so incredibly contagious that if a friend of a friend is happy, you are 10 per cent more likely to be happy, too. Your emotional state depends on other people, many of whom you don't even know.

For a sanuk-filled life, we need to embrace human interaction on a wider scale than we might be used to – or feel comfortable with.

The loneliness epidemic

There's a lot of talk around loneliness in Western society right now, and many of us will experience it at some point. It's something affecting both ends of the age spectrum, with 1 in 10 UK pensioners saying they've had no regular contact or conversation with a friend or relative in more than a month, and 40 per cent of 17- to 25-year-olds admitting they're lonely. In our quest for individuality and independence we haven't realised how much we're giving up by not being connected. The problem was accelerated by the COVID-19 pandemic, as we were confined to home, but even before then, our increasing lack of connection was worrying the UK government so much that, in 2018, they appointed a loneliness minister, the first in the world. Stuart Andrew, the holder of the post at the time of writing, suffered from a sense of isolation growing up gay and feeling unable to tell anyone.

Now he is on a mission to end the stigma around loneliness, telling *The Times*: 'Ten years ago, people would very rarely talk about mental health. Today they'll talk about it openly. I want us to get to the same position on loneliness. I want it to be fine for people to be able to say, "Yes, I'm lonely".'

It's normal to feel lonely at times, and we shouldn't be frightened to admit it. It's not just about being alone; even people who have busy lives, large families and good support networks can find themselves feeling isolated. Whether it's through a relationship breakdown, children leaving home or the loss of support networks when neighbours or friends move away, it happens to young and old alike.

But just because it is common, that doesn't make it any easier. It's so hard to feel sanuk when you are lonely, which makes it all the more important to take action to strengthen connections in all areas of your life. Humans evolved to be around others, and sanuk is a shared experience; it's as much a warm feeling of mutual support and community as it is fun.

CASE STUDY

A sense of belonging –
psychotherapist Noel McDermott

With over 25 years' experience in health and social care, Noel McDermott says the importance of community ties in our physical and mental wellbeing cannot be overstated.

'If people are depressed, they are usually socially isolated,' he notes. 'We're social animals, and if we don't have strong and diverse community around us, we wither on the vine.' The joy of community is that it gives us a wide range of contacts, and it's this variety which is so important. 'When we have a diverse group of people around us, it makes us feel good and produces hormones which make us feel better. While it may be tempting to seek out those who are "just like us", we need a range of views and experiences. Think of it like going to the gym and exercising just one set of muscles.'

This is particularly important for ageing well, as a good social network throughout life increases not just longevity, but quality of life.

'Without it, we see the death of white brain matter (that's the network of nerve fibres that is vital for our health and wellbeing). This loss can lead to dementia and early death,' says Noel, pointing to statistics from the ONS showing that men in Glasgow were dying up to ten years earlier than other men in the UK. 'When they studied the data, they found that one big factor they had in common was that they had no social networks. They were alone. All the research on the impact of loneliness and mortality is showing that it shortens life span.'

Happily, the opposite holds true, too; just as having friends is good for us, we thrive in communities. Social connectedness is a huge factor when it comes to keeping our bodies and minds in good order. People who feel they belong to a group live longer, think clearer and face a lower risk of heart disease than their lonelier counterparts. They're also more optimistic, less depressed and don't feel as anxious. The science couldn't be clearer: a sense of belonging is tied strongly to wellbeing.

When others are lonely

**Knock on the door and
invite them for a cup of tea.**
It could be the only time that they speak
to anybody for weeks. Knowing they are
valued will ease their isolation.

Suggest a fresh purpose.
A new focus can offer new hope and horizons,
whether it's learning a new skill, volunteering or
taking an evening course.

Give your time.
By getting involved with charities dedicated to
reducing loneliness you'll be doing your bit to
tackle it, too. Run to an isolated person's home
for a chat with GoodGym, host a tea party for
older people in your local area with Re-engage or
volunteer on an adventure holiday with disability
charity Sense (see Resources, p. 265).

If *you* feel lonely

Bring back an old hobby.
- something you used to love doing but haven't done in a while; anything from learning to paint again to joining a local choir.

Find the confidence to talk.
Charities who can offer advice by phone include Mind, Silverline and the Samaritans (see Resources, p. 264-5), while your GP can assess your physical and mental wellbeing and provide guidance.

Don't be ashamed.
Being honest with yourself and acknowledging your own emotions is the first step towards combatting isolation.

SANUK TIP
Make conscious decisions: share a smile and chat with the supermarket cashier instead of using the self-service checkout; ask your neighbour how they're doing; check in with a friend you haven't heard from for a while.

Restoring connection

The pandemic has had many lasting effects, but one of the most obvious in our day-to-day lives is convenience at the expense of human connection. Anyone who's tried to pay cash in a shop or café recently will know that pitying look as the contactless card machine is silently offered up instead, without the assistant even making eye contact. Walk into any supermarket and you're more likely to hear that there's an unexpected item in the bagging area than someone asking how your day is going. Computerised call centres and online chat bots leave us in a permanent state of frustration, desperate to talk to someone – anyone! – who can deal with our problem ...

The rush for the money-saving benefits that automation brings comes at a heavy cost. All these so-called advancements are thwarting any opportunity for the pockets of human interaction that break up a day and, in some cases, provide a lifeline in an otherwise isolated life. As we engage in less spontaneous daily chitchat, our conversational skills are suffering as well. Now, you may not think that buying a train ticket or a loaf of bread or even ordering a meal is 'fun', but sanuk is more than having fun; it's about striving to achieve satisfaction and pleasure from whatever you do, and that is impossible without human connection.

There was an interesting debate on the letters page in a British newspaper in the autumn of 2023 which summed up how far away from the spirit of sanuk life can be for some. A reader described how she disliked going to restaurants where she could only access the menu via a QR code and order online. This prompted a reply from someone who said: 'Many people prefer to order food in restaurants online now. It's easier and quicker. Also, I don't know if you've noticed but we don't really want to interact with people anymore – so what a result. Move with the times and stop moaning.'

You don't have to be a people-loving extrovert for your heart to sink when reading this exchange. Daily conversations with friends, family or colleagues or passing the time of day with a stranger are hugely important for our mental health. Ultimately, it comes down to connection and belonging.

One woman who took it upon herself to do something practical to find connection and bring the spirit of sanuk to her neighbourhood is Lyndsey Young. In 2016, she found herself working from home as a freelancer and feeling lonely. When she realised that there was a whole community of lonely people around her, she came up with the idea of

The Friendly Bench® – an outdoor community-led social space with integrated seating for people to meet and take part in events. There's now a network of 15 of these mini-community gardens across England; each The Friendly Bench is independently managed and operated by a local group, and each act as a social hub for anyone feeling isolated, lonely or simply at a loose end. Far more than just a bench, the seating area is built to suit all ages and physical abilities and is a place where visitors can take part in activities, chat and build friendships and a sense of belonging. Cleverly incorporated raised plant beds allow them to connect with nature, too. From an 'aha' moment to a sanuk-filled space, this inspiring social enterprise shows the difference individuals can make to their area – and that it's possible to restore a sense of connectedness to our lives if we're willing to be proactive.

SANUK TIP
Connect with people: it's so hard to have sanuk at home alone – however many 'likes' that photo of your dinner received. Share experiences with others; the more the merrier.

The benefits of volunteering

When we lived on the island of Koh Samui, I'd take a large bin bag with me on my early-morning beach walks and fill it with the discarded bottles and broken glass left in the sand by partying holidaymakers the night before. I did it to stop my young son cutting his feet as he ran into the sea, but just as important was the desire to restore the environment to its pristine beauty. It still astonishes me that people travel thousands of miles to experience a tropical paradise, then feel no obligation to keep it looking that way. But rather than getting depressed, the best solution seemed to play a small part in doing something to help. I'd come back feeling like I'd accomplished something (as well as getting in my steps) – a phenomenon which has been dubbed 'helper's high'. Science shows that when we do something we feel is valuable for the community or for someone else, our brains' pleasure centres light up, releasing endorphins. The buzz we get makes us feel happy, contented and relaxed – an optimum state of sanuk.

A good person takes pleasure in helping others.

Buddha

Performing kind acts from the heart freely and willingly is a big thing in Thai society. They even have a phrase for doing good deeds without expecting reward or praise: 'To put gold leaf on the back of a Buddha statue'. And there's no better way to build a sense of community and form new connections than by volunteering and helping others. As well as being a fantastic opportunity to meet people, it helps to improve your own mental health – studies have consistently demonstrated a link between altruism and wellbeing.

When the big picture seems just too big and overwhelming, making a difference to the immediate world around you can give you a sense of control. Whether it's setting up a communal litter pick, rather than despairing at the rubbish discarded on your streets or joining a campaign to stop the closure of your local library, when you take steps to improve your neighbourhood, you improve your own experience within it and feel more connected to the people around you. Volunteering benefits not only the individual who does it, providing a sense of purpose and meaning, but also their community and society in general. Having a sense of your effect on the lives of others brings with it a powerful sense of sanuk satisfaction. The feelgood feeling it sparks can make you feel better about yourself, making you feel other things are possible. It's a positive spiral whereby the more you help others, the less stressed you are.

DOING GOOD IS GOOD FOR YOU

One US study found that:

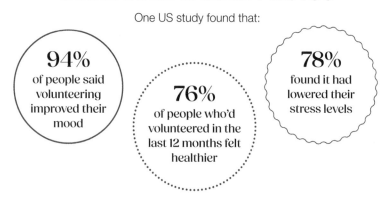

94% of people said volunteering improved their mood

76% of people who'd volunteered in the last 12 months felt healthier

78% found it had lowered their stress levels

The Little Book of Sanuk

Sanuk plus:
five reasons to volunteer

1.
You'll make a difference; your actions can change someone's life for the better.

2.
You'll meet people and build social skills.

3.
Gain self-esteem: doing good for others gives you a sense of accomplishment.

4.
You'll live longer.

5.
It can boost your career; those who volunteer have a better chance of finding a job than those who don't.

The role of empathy in a sanuk life

There's a lot of talk about antisocial behaviour in the news, but very little about prosocial behaviours – essentially, doing things for others' benefit. Thai culture has traditionally taught the importance of these, and in his 2023 New Year speech, King Maha Vajiralongkorn highlighted the fact that kindness and caring for one another is a collective force which binds Thai people together. 'Thais always extend kindness and care and come to the aid of one another in the face of untoward situations,' he said. 'The people are ready and willing to help relieve hardship and despair suffered by others. They work together to prevent and solve difficult circumstances; this is achieved with the good hearts of the people who are kind and empathetic by nature.'

Empathy is understanding how others are feeling and being compassionate towards them. For some, it comes naturally, but you can always be more empathetic. Try spending time with someone you don't know that well and ask them about themselves and what their life is like. On social media, remove yourself from the echo chamber and follow people from many different backgrounds – religious, ethnic, political – and listen to what they have to say.

One can compete in a boat or raft race, but one cannot compete in the race of merit and destiny.

Thai proverb

10 ways to do good

1.
Have a wardrobe clearout and donate clothes you don't wear any more to a charity shop.

2.
Take blankets and duvets you don't use to your local homeless shelter.

3.
Help out at a food bank.

4.
Give away your change.

5.
Mentor a child.

6.
Donate blood.

7.
Do something good for the environment – recycle, use eco-friendly products, reuse.

8.
Pay a compliment to a stranger.

9.
Cook a meal for a friend who's struggling.

10.
Offer to help someone carry their shopping.

A sense of gratitude – Kaz Crossley and the Muay Thai Gym for Kids

Kaz Crossley is a social media influencer who uses her status to make a difference to the lives of children living in poverty in her mum's home country of Thailand. Kaz shares her charity work with her followers, along with her fitness journey through the Thai martial art of Muay Thai. Using her platform, she has helped raise over £100,000 to build a new gym, house and school for at-risk kids to change their path's course.

Her support for the project started when she discovered a Muay Thai boxing club in rural northeast Thailand called Wor Watthana. The community had bought a plot of land but didn't have the funds to build on it. After highlighting their plight on social media, Kaz secured much-needed funds, and is now a regular visitor. Connecting to her mother's Thai heritage and helping the local community has changed the way British-born Kaz looks at the world. She says that in Thailand she is able to live a non-materialistic life, describing it as her happy place. Helping others has had a positive impact on her mental health, too, she explains, paying tribute to the kids' strength and positive attitude: 'The strength they have, the determination and the fact they're so happy and smiling with literally absolutely nothing has completely changed the way I look at life. They push me every day to be grateful and appreciate what we have.' It's a win-win. Doing good for others is a powerful way to boost our own mental health, as well as helping those less fortunate. By actively looking for ways we can help, and acting on them, we can find satisfaction alongside sanuk.

When you do something good, you feel happier. And there's nothing more rewarding than helping the next generation. A sense of happiness and joy is essential for children to reach their full potential, and in the following chapter I'll show how a sanuk-filled childhood can encourage youngsters to discover true contentment for themselves – and make parenthood a happier time for all.

5.

Happy Children

– Dek Mi Kwaam Suk

Children are the future of the nation.

Thai proverb

One of the earliest things which struck me when I first arrived in Thailand was how happy and well behaved the kids were, especially while out shopping. I literally never heard the whine of a child demanding some new toy or screaming toddlers in meltdown mode (essentially, the soundtrack to any UK shopping expedition). We even named our son Siam (the historic name for Thailand) in the hope that some of this would work its magic on him.

It helps that Thai shopping malls encourage a sense of sanuk by having almost as many playgrounds and food halls as shops. Some even have massive swimming pools on the roof. But I've yet to experience a day out there that's turned as noisily sour as so many in the West do … and that's because Thailand's relaxed style of parenting leads to happier and less stressed kids. Just as a sense of sanuk permeates the Thai way of life, so Thai parents work to impart this feeling of carefree *joie de vivre* into their kids.

When Siam was young and we'd visit friends with similar-aged kids in the UK, leaving the house together to go anywhere often turned into an almighty doorway battle between parent and child. Whatever the weather, the scenario was the same: 'Put your coat on.' 'No, I'm not cold.' 'It's cold outside.' 'I don't care, I'm not wearing it.' And on and on … By the time they'd been shoe-horned into their coats, they were in tears, and all the adults were reaching for the wine. What had been intended to be a sanuk outing had turned into a battle of wills, with no winners.

While no Thai parent *ever* has to tell their child to wrap up against the cold (the temperature rarely dips below 25°C), you'll rarely see a similar scenario playing out in Thailand. Their philosophy, unless actual danger is involved, is to let kids get on with it, and they'll soon learn. If they get cold, they'll wear the coat next time. That, in a nutshell, is the sanuk style of parenting. It's about ease, trust, common sense and calm.

Why your 'village' is critical

Despite the fact that Sit and I moved to London when our son Siam was young, our Thai relatives were on hand to help. One day, while Sit and I were both working in London, watching our salaries being swallowed up by sky-high nursery fees, he told me his sister planned to come to England to study and could help. Weird … as far as I knew, Sit only had one sister, Jim, and she was busy raising her own three kids. It transpired that Koong was his younger cousin, but family ties are so close that she was called a sister.

Koong and her friend Tia moved to the UK from Bangkok into our one-bedroom flat. Before I'd spent time in Thailand, the idea of four adults and a baby sharing such a cramped home would have been deeply weird. My London mates certainly thought so. But by this point I'd become accustomed to the idea of communal living, so it seemed worth a go. It helped that Siam adored the attention he got from us all, and the girls were so respectful of our space that after we'd eaten together, they'd take themselves off into the tiny loo to sit and chat while Sit and I put Siam to bed and caught up on our day. Looking back, it seems astonishing, but this money-saving set-up worked for all of us, until Sit and I moved back to Thailand the following year. We're all still close today.

Trying to juggle a job and be there for your family, and never feeling like you're quite getting either 100 per cent right is a problem which almost every working parent grapples with. So much so that one in five mothers of young children has thought about leaving the workforce.

There's nothing particularly sanuk about rushing around, trying to tick parenting boxes, email nurseries, get the week's meals batch-cooked, do the washing, check the homework's done ... For new mums in particular, a strong support network is essential. Studies show that people often feel lonely at a time of life transition, and there's no bigger life shift for women than having a baby. Coupled with the double whammy of changing hormone levels and sleepless nights, no longer having the same social identity can deeply affect our sense of self and make parenthood a lonely time.

We need to reconfigure in a way that helps to prevent a sense of isolation – that's the first step to feeling a sense of sanuk as a parent. As we learned in the previous chapter, for Thai people, life isn't an individual pursuit – and parenting isn't either. Trying to do everything with no support is not a sanuk way to live, as evidenced by the prioritisation of family and community in Thailand. By taking a more collective approach, we have a chance to reconnect to the fun and pleasure which should come with bringing up children. Sharing the experience with friends, family and community means you can create a 'village' in which to raise your children. In the words of this viral Facebook post from community organiser and mother Nakita Valerio: 'Shouting "self-care" at people who actually need community care is how we fail people'.

SANUK TIP

The first step to happier kids is get happy yourself. Have fun with friends or, if you're short on time, think about ways you can still engage in things you enjoy while parenting. If you love reading, listen to an audiobook while you're doing other things.

Four ways for new parents to find a support network

1.

Go online. A digital community can be great for parents of very young children. Awake in the middle of the night breast-feeding or trying to get a little one back to sleep? There's bound to be someone somewhere in the same situation on a parenting Instagram account or Facebook group.

2.

Reach out. There's a reason why new parents gravitate towards one another; they understand the challenges and help each other to find a sense of belonging. If none of your friends has young kids, they may have friends who do, so ask them to put you in contact. Having a friend in common will give you something to talk about apart from your babies, too.

3.

Be proactive. If you see a parent at the playground, strike up a conversation. If they seem like someone you might get on with, ask if they often go there and fancy swapping numbers.

4.

Join a baby-and-me class. Whether it's yoga or an outdoor bootcamp, there are now classes where you can get together with other parents and move your body to get those endorphins going.

Respect for elders

Now that you're not parenting in isolation, you'll find yourself with more time to think about the parent you want to be. There are a few key principles of sanuk parenting, and the first is ensuring your child has gratitude and empathy. As well as making them nicer to be around while they're young, it will also give them crucial life skills to prepare them to be kinder, happier, more sanuk adults.

In Thailand, raising a child to be a good person is a big responsibility. So much so that one of the strongest insults you can give is 'par mac mai sang sort', which means 'your parent has not educated you', because it insults both the person and their parent.

Gratitude to and caring for parents or older people is embedded in Thai culture. With a real sense of the whole family helping to raise the children, rather than it just being up to Mum or Dad, aunts and grannies are often on hand to step in if needed. This extended family makes youngsters feel secure, and they are raised with a deep-seated respect for their elders, bowing their heads as they pass, and doing the

wai – the slight bow with palms pressed together. In restaurants, instead of hordes of kids noisily charging around while their parents feign deafness, everyone sits together and enjoys a sanuk meal. This respect is, remarkably, carried through to the teenage years. On warm Bangkok nights, I still find it amazing to see teens uncomplainingly running errands for their parents.

Kreng jai – sanuk's considerate cousin

Thai parents place great importance on their child being a good person. Inherent in Thai child-rearing is the concept of kreng jai. It literally means awe of heart, and to become a good Thai citizen, you have to kreng jai, or put others first. It's about being aware of people's feelings and showing politeness, respect and consideration towards them; in fact, if you express your own desires too much, you're regarded as a needy person. Kreng jai remains a strong influence into adult life and is a much-admired quality.

Attention please

The child-friendly culture of Thailand means kids get a lot of positive attention and affection from everyone, even strangers. I got a tiny taste of this as a new mum wandering aimlessly through a Bangkok shopping mall, holding baby Siam. I found myself in a silent and very upmarket store, and when one of the immaculate store assistants approached, I froze; the designer outfits were clearly way out of my price range (not to mention lifestyle). Unexpectedly, she smilingly took Siam out of my arms and wandered off, showing him to her colleagues to be admired and cuddled. (He was a very cute baby, but still …)

This sanuk approach and light-hearted, positive affirmation continued throughout his Thai childhood, with so much adoration showered on him I feared he might become arrogant. But I needn't have worried. Rather than spoiling children, praise makes for happier kids. And the more you do it, the more effective it is.

One study by researchers at De Montfort University Leicester (DMU) found that children who are praised by their parents at least five times a day are better behaved, calmer and more attentive than those who are not. Researchers suggested parents 'catch their children being good' and intentionally praise them as a reward. 'It's easy to fall into the trap of paying attention to our children when they are doing something wrong,' they pointed out, 'but we want parents to catch them being good.'

Could there be a nicer, more positive instruction for parents?

Four ways to praise kids

1.

Increase the number of times you praise your children by looking out for when they do something good and saying so.

2.

Describe the good behaviour; when you say exactly what you're happy about, your child knows what you mean and is more likely to repeat it.

3.

Praise effort, rather than ability: children respond better when effort is recognised, rather than achievements.

4.

Instead of waiting until your child does something perfectly, notice little changes and comment on them.

CASE STUDY

Optimistic outlook – Kat Asthana, Thai teacher and content creator

Through her Kat Talks Thai videos on TikTok and Instagram (@Kattoksthai and @kat_talks_thai, respectively), Kat makes learning about Thai language and culture fun for over 300,000 followers. The mum of two is currently based in the USA where, she says, the idea of 'tiger moms' is applied to most Asian parents, 'but that's not the Thai way. It's not tough parenting; Thai parents tend to be gentler. There are still rules in place – respect for parents and teachers is expected – but while there is a push towards education, Thai children don't grow up with a lot of organised activities.'

Kat attributes this more hands-off approach to the positive spirit of sanuk, combined with a dose of optimism that she believes stems from Buddhism. 'We instil in children that they have to have good thoughts and do good deeds in order for good things to happen to them, so parents believe that their children will make good choices. At the same time, we like to have fun, and we're very optimistic in our view of life. Thai people are very laid back. This easy-going, positive outlook means we assume that things will turn out all right.'

Recalling a Thai childhood growing up with lenient parents, Kat says, 'Their approach was "you make your own decisions, and you learn from that". It taught me autonomy and allowed me to make my own choices.' Trusting our children to make mistakes and learn from them is undoubtedly hard, but without the chance to fail they will never learn to overcome disappointment and to keep trying until they succeed.

Let them fail

We all want the best for our kids, but trying to smooth their paths through life can backfire spectacularly. From hovering helicopter parents who micromanage every stage of their children's lives, to lawnmower parents who get rid of any obstacles they see in their paths, we're nurturing a young generation who struggle to develop self-reliance. When a parent is always there to prevent a problem or clean up the mess, kids miss out on the opportunity to learn valuable life lessons from the mistakes they make. Sanuk encourages a focus on the positive – the new way to have fun in any situation. If you never let go, they will never learn to take on responsibilities, and if they never experience failure, they can develop an overwhelming fear of disappointing others. Far better to give them the confidence to try new things and not to feel devastated if they mess up.

How to help your kids cope with life

Psychotherapist Noel McDermott, founder of Mental Health Works, shares what he has learned:

Listen to their opinions. By asking your children questions you teach them that their thoughts and voices are valued and that their opinions matter, meaning they are more likely to come to you if something is bothering them.

Identify emotions. Children have a heap of emotions which are often hard to process, and this can make them emotional without knowing why. Help them identify how they are feeling and why this might be. This will help them to organise their thoughts and normalise them.

Validate feelings. It's ok to feel sad and down; explain to your child that we all have moments when we feel upset and that grown-ups cry, too.

Show empathy. Life is easier for children if they are shown kindness and compassion. Children who grow up with kind and loving parents will develop empathy themselves. Make the time to check in with your child, open up the conversation and give them the chance to connect with you.

Arrange family circle time. Set aside time each week to share feelings in a non-judgemental space. It doesn't have to be a big stress. Once a week after a family meal, spend five minutes going around the table, giving each person some uninterrupted time to check in with their feelings and share them with each other.

Open up real-life, serious conversations. Real-world issues provide great opportunities to put into practice psychological skills; they provoke stress responses, and the better we are at recognising and managing stress, the better our lives will be.

Healthy is happy and happy is healthy. Use activities as an opportunity to show them how being psychologically healthy is the same as having fun. Wellbeing psychologically is no more complex than doing stuff we enjoy, such as having a run around the park; helping your kids understand this simple fact is a gift.

Good enough is good enough

Yes, there are chores to be done, shopping, cooking, cleaning … But with limited time to spend with your kids, what's your parenting goal: keeping a pristine home or spending time with your children and giving them a happy childhood? The good news here is that experts say it's time for us to give ourselves a break. To be a good parent you don't have to be perfect. In fact, it's far better to be simply 'good enough' – the term coined by British paediatrician and psychoanalyst Donald Winnicott back in the 1950s.

Winnicott said that attempting to meet your young child's every need perfectly all the time actually harms their development. That's because being good enough (as opposed to perfect) provides a crucial reality check for kids, which encourages independence and autonomy, as they learn that life can sometimes be a challenge. Winnicott wrote of the good-enough mother: 'Her failure to adapt to every need of the child helps them adapt to external realities. Her imperfections better prepare them for an imperfect world.'

So give yourself a break. In 20 years' time, might you regret being a stressed-out parent who prioritised a spotless home over making time for family life? Create time for some sanuk, and you will all benefit.

SANUK TIP

If you do just one thing … stay calm. Keeping a cool head is valued in Thai culture. If you're about to lose your temper, take a minute to breathe and calm down, or even walk into another room (if it's safe to do so) and come back once you're calmer. You're not avoiding the situation, but you can avoid an impulsive reaction.

Too much too young

Thai parents know that overloading children with material goods isn't the way to happiness. Anyone who's ever witnessed youngsters rip their way through piles of presents, moving on from gift to gift with barely a thank you, will have seen that when children have so much, they can stop seeing the value in things. It's been dubbed the 'abundance paradox': we're more likely to feel disappointed when we don't get what we want than to feel grateful when we do. That gratitude gap yawns all the more widely at Christmas, but it's there throughout the year.

Studies show that children who have fewer material possessions but positive relationships with parents and peers score higher on self-esteem assessment tests. So let's focus on those connections instead.

Create your own Children's Day

One of the most sanuk days of the year in Thailand is Children's Day. Held annually on the second Saturday of January, it's a special time of celebration, an excuse for kids to get centre stage and have fun, with the bonus of cheap or free entry to fun attractions. It's a typically sanuk way to help families bond. Why not create your own personal children's day for you and your kids?

The Little Book of Sanuk

The value of an empty calendar

The diaries of some children are more packed than those of top CEOs. Today's youngsters take part in so many activities designed by adults that it's no longer sanuk for either party. It's time to give them a free rein, without rules or restrictions. Filling kids' agendas from an early age with dozens of extracurricular activities is aimed at helping them prepare for adult life, but rushing around from art classes to music lessons to sports clubs can do more harm than good, allowing less time for true play.

Researchers have found that a busy, organised activity schedule doesn't just put a strain on family relationships and resources but can also potentially harm children's development and wellbeing. Exhausted kids and stressed-out parents are not a sanuk combination. So give yourself permission not to worry about all that stuff … and let them find their own sanuk, their way.

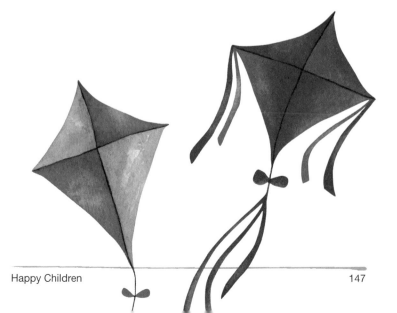

Why play matters

Thais don't like to take things too seriously; on the Internet, for example, you 'len net' which means 'play on the net'. Many activities are prefixed with len (play) to show it isn't a serious activity and is something fun to simply be enjoyed.

If you can still remember the joy of doing what you liked without grown-ups interfering, that's because this 'free play' is the best kind of fun. Outside school, Thai children are free to enjoy playtime without much interference from adults, and this allows them to learn valuable life skills. Playtime isn't just messing around, it's essential for helping kids to grow and learn, says Yesim Kunter, the play expert we met in Chapter 1:

> 'Without play, children are like plants kept in the dark. If they can't play, they can't discover their strengths or find out the risks that they can or can't take. Through play, children learn about the world and their place in it. And the more varied their play, the more they'll learn. When children are relaxed and having fun, they'll quickly soak up these new skills for life without even realising they're doing it.'

Through play, children learn how to: experiment, challenge themselves, learn new skills, share, take turns, make friends, work in groups, negotiate, resolve conflict … So step back, let them have fun and enjoy the process.

If you ask most parents what they want for their kids, the answer is simple: for them to be happy. And that's not just an indulgence, it's a powerful goal – happier kids are more likely to turn into more successful, accomplished adults. When parenting is a battleground, no one wins, but the beauty of sanuk parenting is that it reduces unnecessary conflict, so everyone benefits. It's a style of nurturing which puts the happiness of both parent and child at its heart, with humour used to maintain harmony.

6.

Resilience in the Face of Life's Challenges

– Kwaam Yued Yoon

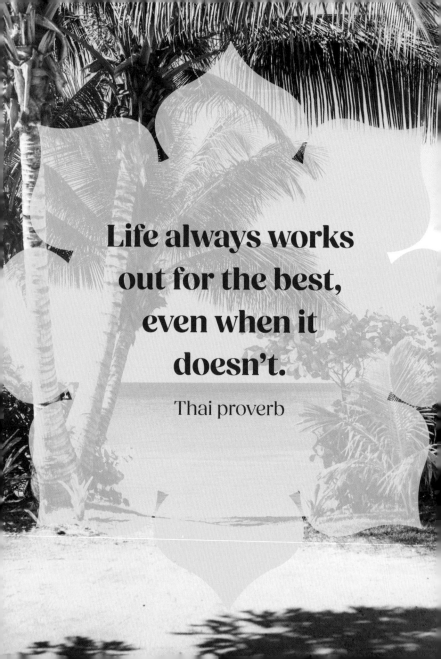

Life always works out for the best, even when it doesn't.

Thai proverb

It's true that sanuk is all about finding joy and pleasure in the everyday, and approaching life with a lightness of spirit, but even when life isn't going how we might want it to, it's still possible to embrace the concept. In fact, sanuk fosters a strong mentality which can help us cope with hardship and smile in the face of adversity.

Resilience in the face of challenges is a quality that allows some people to be knocked down by life and come back at least as strong as before, if not more so. Rather than letting difficulties or failure overcome them and drain their resolve, they find a way to rise from the ashes

This resilience is shown by the entire country of Thailand during monsoon season. Every few years, the nation gets such heavy rains that the streets flood and cities can become criss-crossed with rivers. News reports show belongings floating down the roads, the elderly being rescued with makeshift boats and entire communities relocating to drier land. But look at the photos and one thing strikes you: whether they're a septuagenarian being rowed to safety in a canoe or kids wading through waist-deep waters, all those people have one thing in common – they're all still smiling.

This response is partly down to their happy-go-lucky and cheerful disposition, but also due to the Thai philosophy that if you express open anger or sadness, you can create bad feelings in other people. And while it is bad enough to feel strong emotion yourself, it's much worse to cause that in others. Thais value consideration and think of others' feelings before their own. Far better to smile, whatever the circumstance, and do your best to bring good karma to all.

In Thailand, there is less emphasis on the future and more on what is going on today, right now. In a world where we are increasingly concerned about the future, there is something refreshing about just looking at today and concentrating on the concerns of the moment, rather than fretting about what might happen next week or next year.

Thailand's extraordinary cave rescue

The Thai attitude of courage, resilience and community is something that the whole world saw in the summer of 2018. There was one news story which gripped everyone around the globe. Twelve young boys and their football coach had entered caves in northern Thailand to explore and became trapped inside by sudden rains. It was almost too much to comprehend. Even if rescuers did manage to find them, how would the boys – aged just 11–16 – have coped, not just with the terror of being entombed with no food or drink, but also with the silence and darkness?

Almost unbelievably, after more than two weeks, they were freed, unharmed, having survived on rainwater dripping down the cave rocks and meditation, which helped them remain calm and preserve their energy. As they smilingly thanked their rescuers, it emerged that their coach, Ekapol 'Ek' Chanthawong, had lived in a Buddhist monastery for a decade and taught them to meditate. At 23, he was not much older than his charges, but his actions helped turn their ordeal into a tale of resilience.

When they were successfully brought out of the cave, the boys were ordained as novice monks and spent over a week living at a Buddhist temple to fulfil a prayer that their families made in exchange for their safe return, as well as to honour a volunteer diver who died while saving them.

This sense of gratitude played an important part in the families' response. In the West, there might have been recriminations and even threats of lawsuits. But instead, the parents expressed their thanks to Ek for caring for their sons. Rather than anger and blame, they showed compassion and forgiveness; they wanted to get on with their lives and let the coach do the same. He has done just that and has since set up a football academy to help young Thai children reach their potential.

It's how we face challenges that determines how we transcend hardship, and the spirit of optimism and the social bonds fostered by sanuk played a huge part in how the schoolboys were able to cope at the time. From the Buddhist meditation that kept them calm in the cave to the boys' strong social connections with one another, key factors that promote resilience are ingrained in the spirit of sanuk.

Sanuk in sadness

The Thai tradition to temporarily ordain as a novice monk is something sons often do after the death of a parent. It's not just a way to express appreciation for their care, it's an excuse for friends and family to get together to remember lost loved ones and have sanuk. When my brother-in-law, Meuk, did this after his father, Prasat, passed away, there was an all-night street party, head shaving and musical procession through the area to see him off. When he came home, a few weeks later, another party was thrown to welcome him back. It's possible to find sanuk in sadness, too.

Mai pen rai – acceptance through sanuk

Deeply connected to sanuk is the Thai concept of 'mai pen rai' – the acceptance of what cannot be changed. This relates to the Thai cultural conviction that people don't have much control over things. The belief that everything will be fine, and there is no point stressing about what you can't control, allows space for acceptance of whatever might be happening. In other words, what will be will be, so go with the flow. Studies show that this is a proven way to resilience. The key to helping yourself psychologically is to recognise that there is little you can do about events, so your focus needs to come to what you can have an influence over, which is generally yourself and your immediate family.

SANUK TIP

Do the best you can with what you have and accept what you cannot change.

Rethinking resilience

A typical way to describe resilience is the ability to bounce back from troubles. However, a study looking at the concept of resilience in rural Thai older people in the face of adversity concluded that 'bouncing back' didn't really apply. A more apt phrase would be 'moving on'. Researchers noted: 'Bouncing back implies a setback, whereas "moving on" is the process of continuous movement forward and getting on with one's life despite difficulties.' Sanuk is concerned with a focus on the positives; Thai people instinctively know that dwelling on past traumas serves no purpose and that in a bad situation, there can still be something good. They even have a phrase for this: chua jet tee dee jet hon – bad seven times, good seven times. Resilience is not developed through succeeding and winning, it's developed through surviving loss and trauma, getting up again, and taking what we can learn from the situation as a positive.

Six ways to nurture resilience

Learning to manage and bounce back from life's challenges doesn't happen overnight. But by following this advice, taken from the NHS Tips For Life, in time you might notice that you start to work through these steps automatically – and by doing so, you will boost your chance of a sanuk-filled life.

1. Start with what you're good at

Thinking about something you're good at, big or small, can help you to recognise your skills and abilities. Maybe you play a team sport, cook or garden? Are you a caring friend or parent – what makes you good at it? Does it take patience? Organisation? Compassion? If you need help to identify your strengths, consider an average day: which parts do you find easier? What tasks do you feel more confident doing?

2. Think about difficulties you have overcome

Even the things we are good at can come with difficulties. Take the activity or trait from step 1 and remember times that were harder or required a change in your approach. How were you able to overcome it? Maybe you prepared a complicated meal by reading the recipe beforehand and breaking it down into manageable chunks. What can you learn from this earlier situation that might help you with other challenges now and in the future?

3. See how you can apply this elsewhere

Now think about how these positive traits could be applied to other, more challenging areas of your life. For example, knowing how to manage your time when cooking could mean you have the skills to manage your time at work when things feel busy. Being a caring friend could mean you have good listening skills, which could help you to resolve conflict in other areas of your life. Repeat this exercise whenever you face a challenge.

4. Find an image or metaphor to help you in difficult times

Changing the way you think about a situation can be a big help, especially when a challenge feels too difficult at first. Using images or metaphors can have a positive impact on how you feel. Think about how a DJ can change the mood in the room instantly with the choice of track. If you're struggling to start or complete a task, imagine you're out and the DJ has just changed the music to your favourite upbeat tune. Would this give you a burst of energy to keep going? Can you use this example and apply it to your difficult time?

5. Plan ahead

If you find yourself feeling overwhelmed, find 5 or 10 minutes to sit in a quiet place and problem solve. This may be easier with a pen and paper, or recording yourself speaking. Use the previous four tips to help you come up with strategies for working through challenges. Think about these questions:

What are the issues I am facing?
What actions do I need to take first?
Which strategies have I used in the past that can help me now?
Can I look at this situation in a different way?

6. Reflect, recognise and reward

Take some time each month to reflect. Think about the challenges you've faced and how you dealt with them, making sure you take the time to recognise and celebrate your achievements. Mark the moment by rewarding your achievements with an activity you really enjoy.

CASE STUDY

From despair to hope – Ani Naqvi

In Christmas 2004, Ani Naqvi's world was literally turned upside down when she narrowly survived the devastating tsunami that took almost a quarter of a million lives in seconds, including thousands in Thailand.

She was on holiday when she awoke in her beach hut just before 9am, suddenly aware of a commotion. 'I heard loud sounds and a low roar,' she recalls. 'Still half asleep, I couldn't understand what the noise was – and then, suddenly, the sea crashed into the room, ripping the door off its hinges, tearing my clothes off, raising me off the bed like a doll. In the split second it took for me to come to, I was under water. It was like being a grain of rice thrown around in a washing machine. The sheer force of the water made it impossible to swim, and everything was pitch black. The concrete hut started to fill with water, furniture smashed into me, and I tried desperately to make out which way was up.'

After a harrowing fight for her life, Ani finally made it to higher ground, but like so many other survivors, she found herself in the throes of

post-traumatic stress disorder, suffering crippling survivor guilt. Six years later, while still in her 30s, a diagnosis of cancer led her to turn to yoga, meditation, mindfulness and the alternative-medicine system Ayurveda to help her manage the extraordinary challenges that life was throwing at her.

Now, cancer-free, she travels the world as a motivational speaker, sharing her journey from despair to hope. Through her coaching work, Ani inspires others to make a positive impact and live their lives with purpose and joy, saying, 'I wouldn't be the person I am today without all of the challenges I've faced. Every challenge is an opportunity for our growth. What if, in our darkest hour we find our greatest strengths?'

Ani says her meditation and mindfulness training was key in enabling her to switch from simply surviving to thriving: 'Resilience isn't about avoiding difficulties; it's about developing the inner strength to navigate them. By embracing the practice of being present, we can strengthen our mental and emotional wellbeing, allowing us to face life's storms with grace and composure.'

Over the page, Ani shares two simple techniques we can all use every day. These will help you find calm in the moment and allow space for sanuk.

Exercise 1:
Embracing the breath

1. Find a quiet, comfortable place to sit. Ensure your head, neck and spine are straight, allowing for free and easy breathing.

2. Softly close your eyes. This allows you to turn your attention inwards, focusing solely on your inner world.

3. Inhale slowly and deeply to a count of four, directing your breath towards your belly and diaphragm. Feel your abdomen gently rise and expand.

4. Exhale slowly and deeply for eight counts. Allow your breath to flow out smoothly and steadily.

5. Keep your attention anchored to the breath. Feel the rhythm of each inhale and exhale, the ebb and flow of this life-giving force.

6. When your mind wanders, acknowledge the wandering thought, and then gently guide your focus back to the breath. The breath serves as a bridge between the mind and the body. As you slow it down, you'll notice the mind naturally quieting. This calming effect allows you to tap into a deeper sense of stillness and presence.

Exercise 2:
One-minute mindfulness

Take one to two minutes every hour to focus on one physical sensation, such as touch or sound (see below). This helps move the mind's focus to present-moment awareness of physical sensations and serves as a fundamental building block in mindfulness and meditation practices. Integrating these into your daily routine helps to shift your brain from survival mode to thriving and, in turn, builds resilience and enhances your mental agility. Taking just a few moments every hour to engage in these exercises fosters a continuous state of present-moment awareness and activation in the creative, problem-solving hemisphere of the brain.

Touch – Gently rub two fingertips together, fully immersing yourself in the tactile sensations. Do it so slowly and with such attention that you notice the ridges of your fingertips, the temperature of your skin.

Sound – Focus intently on the distant sounds around you or simply observe the rhythmic rise and fall of your chest or stomach with each breath.

Pulling together

There's no doubt that life can be stressful. But anxiety runs high in the modern age, even as 'real' danger has subsided. 'As a society we work extraordinarily well to survive and thrive through challenge, and human society is so much greater than the sum of its parts,' says psychotherapist

Noel McDermott. 'Have belief and faith in the future. It's easier to avoid stressful and frightening events but, in fact, there is a lot of personal growth available through overcoming struggle and adversity. Celebrate your resilience and connection to loved ones, family and friends.'

COVID-19 hit Thailand hard, and while the numbers of deaths were mercifully low (under 35,000, compared to Britain's 232,112), with strict travel restrictions in place, an economy reliant on tourism suffered, as did the lives of the many Thais who work in the industry. Tourism has a workforce of about 4 million, including lots of my family and friends, and it bore the brunt of the impact. But when researchers came to look at how Thai people handled the crisis, they found that the pandemic led to the resurgence of traditional values of empathy and community feeling, and the strong connections of Thais helped them cope. Solidarity among the Thai people was a key contributing factor to the country's resilience during the pandemic, with family, community and local networks all playing a part in supporting people.

And that's the point. We will inevitably go through periods of pain and trauma, but these moments can be weathered if we have good relationships. Ultimately, it's the strength of our bonds that determines everything. Sanuk encourages good relationships with those around us, and accepting help and support from those who care gives us the ability to see past problems, find enjoyment in life and handle stress better. It's a far more positive approach than trying to avoid anything which might upset us. In fact, some studies are showing that the modern-day trend for trigger warnings, designed to alert us that the content we are about to consume might be disturbing, may, in fact, be counterproductive. Our obsession with protecting each other has made us more vulnerable and is damaging our sense of resilience.

Life is not without pain – physical or mental – and we all need to learn to cope as best we can. And this is where sanuk can help. Appreciating small moments helps us to feel gratitude for where we are now and to see the world in a more positive light. Humour is proven to reduce the threatening nature of stressful situations, so by embracing the spirit of sanuk, we can increase resilience and the capacity to tolerate stress.

Holding on to hope

Resilience is about understanding the difference between fate and freedom, learning to take responsibility for our own lives and working within our scope of control. There will always be challenges beyond our control, but it's how we respond to them that helps us cope.

SANUK TIP

If you can find a way to integrate more fun into your life, you will unlock your full potential, and be better equipped to tackle the challenges that life throws your way.

You can't change the past, but you can always look towards the future. An optimistic outlook enables you to expect that good things will happen in your life. Sanuk comes with a spirit of hope which builds resilience. Accepting the inevitable changes life brings will make it easier to adapt and help you to view new challenges with less fear and more optimism.

7.

Enjoy Working

– Tam Ngan Sanuk

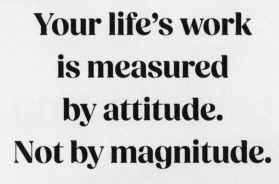

Your life's work is measured by attitude. Not by magnitude.

Thai proverb

When I find myself back working in the UK after spending time in Thailand, the first thing I notice is how stressed and miserable my fellow commuters on the train look. The way we work seems to be making us more stressed and more ill with every passing day; but it doesn't need to be this way – while Thais have a strong work ethic, they don't believe that working hard equals misery.

It's been suggested that the idea of sanuk may be rooted in Thailand's agricultural past, when the long days working in rice fields or on the land were livened up with songs, jokes, teasing and gossip. Whatever its origins, although Thai people may work longer hours than in the West, the work is approached differently. In fact, work and relaxation are not necessarily viewed as opposites. It's not that work isn't carried out efficiently, rather that it's done with a relaxed attitude that pervades entire workplaces. To rush and stress over work is simply not considered a good way to get things done in Thailand.

Whatever their job, Thai people will try and make it sanuk. And they generally succeed. My Thai friends say that the best-functioning offices in Bangkok are ones in which work is treated like a social activity. The spirit of sanuk is so embedded in Thais' work life that they have a phrase for it: sanuk gap tam ngaan – to work and to enjoy working. It's boring made fun, daily business turned entertaining and the whole process worth a laugh. When pressure gets too much, it's a way of lightening the mood. So given that we can spend an estimated 90,000 hours at work in a lifetime, in this chapter, we'll be looking at ways we can all get some of the sanuk spirit into our working lives.

Connection at work

The collective nature of Thai culture continues into the workplace. Teamwork is key. The emphasis on group consensus and achieving common goals means that personal relationships and building rapport are considered essential. A concept central to Thai society is gan eng – each other, together. It's the spirit of togetherness in work and then in play. No wonder that according to a poll by the National Institute of Development, 92 per cent of Thai workers say they have a very happy or happy work life, compared with 27 per cent of UK workers (based on Indeed's Work Happiness Score).

As we move forward in a post-pandemic world, it's time to try to figure out a new way of working which brings sanuk for us all. The shift to hybrid and remote has changed the way many of us experience employment. Working from home has permanently altered the landscape, but with no clear distinction between work and home, workdays can bleed into semi-working evenings where fun is in short supply.

This flexibility is also leading to an increased disconnect from one another – there are far fewer opportunities for communal lunches when lots of people aren't working from the office. We are a profoundly social species, and being away from colleagues can leave people feeling isolated. It's an evolutionary throwback –

SANUK TIP

There's a time to be serious, but it's still possible to inject some fun into working life. Humour helps to reduce anger and anxiety, so instead of constantly complaining, be the reason a colleague smiles today.

humans evolved to be in groups together and when social creatures are deprived of social contact, they feel like they are missing out. We may save travel costs and be able to fit work more easily into our lifestyles, but it comes at a cost. For some, working at home is just not a sanuk way to spend the day.

Thai workers certainly think so. In a recent survey by Robert Walters Inc., one third said that one of the main downsides of working from home was the lack of socialising with colleagues. They missed the sanuk that comes with spending days with others. Worryingly, this could be rewiring our brains, too, which are largely developed for socialisation. What might seem to be simply a water-cooler chat can stimulate attention and memory and help to strengthen neural networks.

To restore a sense of sanuk, the answer is not to simply go back to the way things were. Employee attitudes have shifted. For every boss walking around an expensive empty building and wondering why they pay the rent, there are employees asking why they should go to the office at all. Instead, companies need to create an environment where collaboration, cooperation and shared responsibilities are all encouraged to foster a sense of community – whether at home or in the office.

This concept isn't new, but while most businesses recognise the value of collaborative working, not all of them have figured out how to do it right. Architect Erin Peavy has trained in psychology and is interested in how to design work environments to combat loneliness and create a sense of belonging. 'Social health, or the way we connect with others, has huge impacts on our mental and physical health, and our ability to think clearly and be productive, positive members of a team,' she notes.

To Erin, hybrid working allows for the best of both worlds. For while increased flexibility allows a better work–life balance, too much time spent working from home can lead to a feeling of being separate from your colleagues. 'Being in person helps deepen connections, especially informal ones, that create the ability to bond to one another on things other than work. Over time, colleagues build trust that translates to friendships, and becomes a social lubricant that can smooth workplace interactions.'

To create an environment which encourages creativity, think about paint, light, nature, and texture as your friends, says Erin. 'Any time you can create "working walls" – whiteboards or pin-up boards where people can share ideas you are creating a sense of increased belonging in that space,' she adds. 'Much of our work lives are marked by formality, so if there are ways to create a space that helps people to feel more informal – space to get outside, to be more playful, this can help create moments of sanuk in your working day.'

There are some other easy wins, such as ensuring there are enough meeting rooms and communal spaces where people can gather to discuss projects easily. But it's not just physical. For collaboration to flourish, the culture needs to promote it. When you have a mistrustful boss who scowls every time you leave your workstation, you'll struggle to feel relaxed enough to share ideas.

Research shows that we thrive in environments which free us to communicate and work together, so if you're stuck with a manager who can't let go of the old way of thinking, it's worth starting a conversation about how you can all learn from each other. It might help them to know that everyone benefits; one study found that those who work together are not just more motivated and engaged, but 50 per cent more effective at completing tasks.

Let's do lunch

The spirit of togetherness is never more obvious than when it comes to food. Rather than joylessly consuming a shop-bought sandwich at their desks or on their own in the staff room, Thai workers will head out to their favourite restaurant or noodle stall for lunch with colleagues. It's not just a tastier and more pleasurable way of eating – making time for lunch outside of work keeps people together and fosters strong social bonds. The sanuk result? Happier, more productive and collaborative teams.

Thai cultural observer Kat Asthana, who we met in Chapter 5, currently lives in Austin, Texas, where she sees a very different approach to the working day. 'For people in the US, lunches are a functional means to an end,' she says. 'In Thailand, that's your social break and you barely skip it. Lunch is a big thing; you make time to go out and bond with colleagues while eating. And that one action, just the act of eating, is in itself already sanuk.' People often socialise together outside of work, too, Kat adds. 'There's a camaraderie within the company environment; people work hard and play hard together. Your co-workers become your friends.' Sanuk fosters this sense of fellowship; the group is always more important than the individual.

If you still draw a blank at the top, there's nothing to stop you working with colleagues at a local level. Suggest a brain-storming session over lunch or stay on after a group video call to see if anyone has extra ideas they didn't manage to mention on the call.

Author and psychotherapist Eloise Skinner, whose work focuses on existential therapy, suggests getting a sense of purpose by being a workplace mentor or coach for someone less experienced. 'Joy and happiness are often found in giving back, or in acts of service,' she says. 'Volunteer for mentoring programmes – if your company doesn't have this sort of scheme, then start one. Or take a junior colleague out for a coffee to answer any questions they have. Suggest regular catch-ups with junior team members; even spending a few extra moments providing feedback or advice to a colleague can deliver a sense of fulfilment and purpose.'

Create added sanuk by forming a social committee to ensure that something fun is always happening. Building strong relationships at work won't just benefit your career – it can increase moments of joy in your day, too.

SANUK TIP

There's lots to be gained by hanging out with the people you work with. They can help solve problems – or be a shoulder to cry on if they turn out to be unsolvable.

Work and play – Kulthirath Pakawachkrilers, entrepreneur

When it comes to making the working day sanuk, human connection is key, says Kulthirath, co-founder and CEO of digital consulting firm Thailand e-Business Center (TeC).

'The collectivist nature of Thai society extends to the workplace,' she explains. 'Thais value the collective success of the team or organisation over individual achievement.'

With loyalty and trust key drivers, teamwork is highly regarded because it contributes to the overall harmony and success of the group, and is an opportunity to enjoy sanuk. 'Thais prioritise positive social interactions in the workplace because friendly conversations, sharing a sense of humour and fostering good relationships with colleagues can make the workday more enjoyable,' Kulthirath says.

With a strong emphasis on food and celebrations, whether it's free snacks, lunch to celebrate a birthday or hitting a sales target, socialising in and outside the workplace is important. It doesn't just provide a break from routine work, it helps to build a sense of belonging.

'These moments of joy and togetherness contribute to a positive work culture,' says Kulthirath. 'People on the team trust each other more, get along better, and feel like they fit.'

Music-loving Thais often have the latest hits playing in the workplace, as well as regular karaoke outings, and their relaxed and easy-going approach to life contributes to a sense of work sanuk, says Kulthirath.

'Thais tend to have a playful sense of humour and enjoy joking and teasing with colleagues,' she adds. 'Light-hearted banter and humour can be an integral part of the work culture, helping people feel less stressed and the atmosphere positive and peaceful.'

While sanuk can't ace a job interview for you, it can help you enjoy the job you have. By taking active steps to lighten the mood, bond with others and share jokes, you'll bring moments of joy to each working day, no new CV required.

It's not about gimmicks

We've all heard of tech start-ups whose offices are try-hard attempts to inject a quirky sense of fun into the working day: swings hanging from the ceiling acting as chairs, desks made from old wooden doors propped up on breeze blocks, bright red slides and table tennis (of course) … More and more employers are following the trend set by companies such as Google towards a more interactive and less formal office, but without the Silicon Valley budget or expertise, things don't run quite so well. Even the most creative and nimble millennial finds it hard to work in that environment.

Making a workplace more fun doesn't mean creating a space that doubles as a playground. It can be as simple as providing drinks and snacks which encourage kitchen gatherings where co-workers get to know each other better.

I've worked in a few offices over the years, and although there have been moments of stress and boredom along the way, I've found sharing highs and lows with others hugely bonding. Job cuts of 25 per cent across the company? Meet you in the pub. A new CEO? Who's got any inside intel? Some of my closest friends are ex-colleagues, but I've also had sanuk with many others over the years. We may not have stayed in touch, but from champagne-fuelled evenings at award ceremonies to fleeting corridor chats about our latest Netflix obsessions, I treasure countless sanuk memories.

Having friends in the workplace can not only boost job satisfaction and performance, but also improve wellbeing. When someone steps in to help you on a busy day, or shares advice and opinions, this can buffer the negative effects of stress. It's linked to a lower risk of burnout, better mental health, fewer traumatic experiences and maybe even a longer lifespan. The goal isn't necessarily to make life-long friends –

although it's great if you do – but rather, to foster 'a sense of being in the right place' by becoming part of a community with a larger purpose, says Kim Samuel, author of *On Belonging: Finding Connection in an Age of Isolation*. The view of work as a place to find fulfilment rather than just earn money is a new one, she points out, writing in *MacLeans* magazine – 'More and more managers will have to build bonds by controlling less and listening more.' Workplace connections are important not just to people, but to the global economy, with workers who are lonely being less productive and less motivated, as well as more likely to leave their jobs. Simple things like encouraging employees to eat together and take breaks at the same time can go a long way towards alleviating this problem.

You'll soon start to reap the rewards of finding the fun in your work and when you're working with a sunnier, sanuk outlook everyone benefits. Happy employees are better and more productive and less likely to quit. Strong connections help people communicate better and relaxed working environments stimulate open discussion and trust.

10 ways to work sanuk

1.

Make an effort to connect with some people you work with. Colleagues may not be your friends, but you spend enough time with them for the effort to be worth it.

2.

If workplace moaning saps your energy, then pull back from it, as it can be contagious.

3.

It's not fun being the new person, so go the extra mile to be supportive, even if it's just to share a good place to get lunch.

4.

Show your appreciation for something a colleague did, even if it was part of their job.

5.

Celebrate successes and milestones, whether it's a company achievement or your colleague's birthday.

6.

Value other people's skills, especially if they are different from yours.

7.

Set up a gratitude wall where people can post messages to those who've positively influenced their work life.

8.

Go out together as a team – it's a great way to get everyone having fun and key to forming a collaborative culture. Organised outings such as paintball games build connections between bosses and workers.

9.

Start an office book club.

10.

Eat lunch anywhere but at your desk.

Switch off

Sanuk is in short supply when we feel overworked and stressed, so scheduling downtime is vital in an age where the line between work and leisure is increasingly blurred. Eight in 10 employees say that work–life balance is key when looking for their next role. For centuries, we mainly did manual jobs in a fixed place we could leave. Today, cognitive tasks can follow us around after hours, says Claire Neal, head of workplace mental health at Mental Health UK. She warns, in *The Times*: 'People are just not putting boundaries in place and recharging their batteries.' The 24/7, 'always on' working culture is stopping people switching off properly, so in the same way that manual workers down tools when the job's done, we should all turn off laptops and disable work emails at the end of the day.

Tough times

If, despite your best efforts, work is still difficult – if, say, you have to deal with a toxic boss – give it a sanuk spin and look for the good in the situation. Take the positive from it, which is that this person is showing you how not to be a good leader. Not only that, learning to work with difficult people will teach you invaluable life skills and help to strengthen a core of mental resilience, which will serve you well when facing future challenges. If you shift your attitude to one of growth, rather than irritation, you can reframe challenging people as a learning experience.

Your support network of friends, family and other colleagues can be valuable for helping you get through a challenging situation; they may have been in a similar situation and can offer advice.

If it's your job as a whole that you hate, look at it as a valuable opportunity to realise what you don't want. In the meantime, perhaps you can find humour in your day? Enjoying a moment of camaraderie with co-workers or celebrating a small win can boost team spirits. Workmates can also be invaluable in helping to identify what you're best at, which is vital in increasing job satisfaction.

'Play to your strengths,' advises Eloise Skinner. 'At work, we can sometimes feel like our everyday tasks are out of our control. Try "job tailoring": figure out which parts of your job you excel at, or which bring you most fulfilment and joy, and tailor your work in this direction. This could mean volunteering for new projects, suggesting new initiatives or just performing your preferred tasks to the best of your ability. Over time, you might be able to shift your overall focus in the direction that delivers the most joy.'

And if it's really not working out, make a plan for the future. As Eloise says, 'Finding happiness in the present moment can often be related to having a strong sense of purpose or vision about where you'd like things to head in the future. Craft a work-related vision statement for yourself. List your biggest, most intimidating goals for your career future, then work back through each one, breaking it into practical and shorter-term steps. Once you have your goal in manageable sections, figure out one or two actions you can take every week to make a move towards it. Hold yourself accountable – check back in regularly and remind yourself of the progress you've made so far.'

Stressed out?
Five ways to deal with work tension

It's a rare job that doesn't come with the occasional challenge, but these strategies, from the New Economics Foundation and mental health charity Mind, offer ways to deal with work tension (see Sources, page 269).

1. Connect

Connecting with others can help us feel close to people, and valued for who we are. Try these:

- Speak to someone new.
- Ask how someone's weekend was, and really listen when they tell you.
- Put five minutes aside to find out how a colleague is doing.

2. Get active

Getting active can help you to sleep better and reduce feelings of stress and anxiety. Try these:

- Take the stairs, rather than the lift.
- Go for a walk at lunchtime.
- If you're in the office, walk over to someone's desk instead of calling or emailing.

3. Take notice

Savouring the moment can also help you to feel more positive about life. Try these:

- Get a plant for your workspace.
- Have a 'clear-the-clutter' day.
- Visit a new place for lunch.

4. Learn

Feeling like you're learning and developing can boost your self-esteem. Try these:

- Set up a book club.
- Do a crossword or Sudoku.
- Research something you've always wondered about.

5. Give

People who help others are more likely to rate themselves as happy. Is there anything you can do today to be kind or helpful to someone else? Try these:

- Make a cup of tea for a colleague.
- Offer to help a workmate with something they're stuck on.
- Introduce yourself to a new starter, to help them feel more at ease.

8.

Wellbeing

– Kwaam Suk Sabai

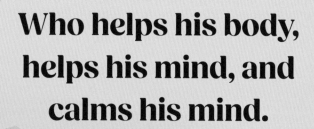

Who helps his body, helps his mind, and calms his mind.

Thai proverb

In Thailand, wellness is not a trend, it's rooted in the culture. Holistic and spiritual healing are part and parcel of Thai daily life and have been for centuries. Besides curing diseases and ailments, the primary goal of traditional Thai medicine is maintaining health and wellbeing. Today, spas in Thailand tune into this long history with therapeutic massage and relaxation exercises, the use of medicinal herbs and a conscious diet, all combined with a culture of sanuk to help ease body and mind – and they're world-renowned for doing so.

Sanuk can be in short supply when you feel physically run down, so Thailand always serves as a health reset for my family. One of the first things we do is to head off for the first of many massages. What is an expensive occasional treat in the UK is an affordable part of day-to-day wellbeing for Thais. Whether it's a quick back-and-shoulder massage in a street market to ease out the kinks from our long flight, or a 90-minute full-body experience, we emerge feeling brighter, freer and more energised … and keen to go back for more.

The spa capital of the world

Thailand is ranked the top country in the world for wellness retreats and has something for everyone, all performed with a smile. Want to get fit? Lose weight? Destress? Cleanse and detox? Not talk for a week? There's a retreat with your name on it …

Thai massage

Thai people maintain a healthy balance between work, leisure and self-care, and massage is embedded in daily life. As well as massage shops and parlours on almost every street, Thai people give each other shoulder, neck and feet massages in the home to help them relax. The preparation starts early, with toddlers being encouraged to walk across their parents' backs as they lie on the floor to ease aching muscles. We trained Siam to do this when he was young, and it's an incredibly sanuk experience for both parties. It was a sad day when he got too big and heavy to continue.

> You can't walk a mile in another person's shoes. But you can massage their feet.
>
> Thai proverb

An ancient healing method that's been practised for thousands of years, Thai massage has its roots in India and is based on the yogic principles of invisible lines of energy, or prana, that run through the body. It uses passive stretching and gentle pressure along these energy lines to increase flexibility, relieve muscle and joint tension, as well as balance the body's energy systems. The health benefits include boosting circulation, stress relief, better sleep, help with headaches and improved flexibility.

Dubbed by some as the 'lazy person's yoga', traditional Thai massage (also known as Nuad Thai) does require a bit more active participation than other types of massage as it involves some yoga-like stretching. In the past, villages had massage healers for locals with muscle aches from working in the fields; now it's considered so important it's been added to the UNESCO heritage list of intangible cultural heritage practices.

CASE STUDY

What to expect in a Thai massage – Kattalin 'Kat' Buasrichan, Thai massage therapist and trainer

For anyone who's never been for a traditional Thai massage, Kat, director of Thai Therapy Massage, says: 'Thai massage is carried out fully clothed, and can be done on the floor, a firm mattress or a mat. We don't use oils or lotion. Wear loose, comfortable clothes that won't restrict your movements because your therapist will be moving you into different positions and stretches.

'It's a deep, full-body treatment which starts at the feet and progresses up to the head using a sequence of gentle, flowing exercise movements. You start on your back, and your massage therapist will gently push and pull your limbs to stretch and release muscles, so lie back and trust in them. We use our hands, knees, legs and even our feet to manipulate your body into a series of yoga-like poses. Stretching, pulling and rocking techniques help to relieve tension and enhance flexibility.

'The techniques are based on the belief that tight muscles diminish the flow of energy. When the body's energy is immobile, stiffness and inflexibility create discomfort and pain. Although you may feel sleepy straight after a Thai massage, it ultimately restores the flow of energy throughout the body by unblocking and balancing the body's energy pathways.'

Blind massage

Massage given by blind or visually impaired practitioners is a sought-after treatment in Thailand. One of Sit's friends, Ning, was a beauty therapist, until she lost her sight in an accident. Channelling the Thai philosophy of mai pen rai – what will be, will be – she now runs a massage business where all the therapists are blind. With no visual cues, and a heightened sense of touch and feeling, blind therapists are said to be more in tune with the body's responses. Certainly, Ning found knots and areas of tension in areas I didn't even know I had ...

Stretch out

As you now know, stretching is a key element of Thai massage; after all, there's nothing sanuk about being stiff and immobile. It's vital to maintain flexibility as we age, and Thai people stretch little and often. Performed daily, the wellbeing stretching exercises below from Eleonora Sansoni (osteopath and co-founder of Wellthy Clinic, London) will help aid flexibility.

1. Standing roll down
Relieves back tension and stretches your legs.

Stand with your back to a wall, aligning the back of your head, spine and sacrum firmly against it and your feet slightly away. Lower your chin towards your chest and drop your head forward first, then your

The Little Book of Sanuk

shoulders. Continue to roll your spine down and, feeling your lower back pushing the wall, let your head and arms hang freely. Roll down as far as you feel comfortable, until you experience a gentle stretch in the backs of your legs or spine. Reverse the roll down, coming up one vertebra at a time, until you have returned to the starting position. Repeat 6–8 times.

If this exercise causes strain to your neck, lower back or shoulders, reduce your range of motion and work only within a pain-free range.

2. Hamstring stretch

Improves calf and hamstring flexibility and leg range of motion.

Lie flat on your back with your left leg straight down and your right leg bent. Lift your right leg into a tabletop position. Place a long, rolled-up towel under the sole of your right foot and hold the ends of the towel with both hands. Extend your right knee to lengthen your right leg straight up. Flex your right knee. Repeat 6–8 times. Repeat on the left side.

3. Thread the needle

A deep, gentle stretch to open your shoulders, chest, neck and back. Kneel on your hands and knees, knees under hips, hands under your shoulders, and head and neck lifted in alignment with your spine. Reach your right arm down and under your left shoulder. As you move, allow your spine to rotate and stretch through your left side as far as it feels comfortable. Once you reach the end of your range, hold the position for two seconds and return to the start position. Repeat the exercise 12 times, alternating sides.

If you experience any discomfort in your shoulders or back, reduce the range of motion.

The Little Book of Sanuk

Two basic techniques for self-massage

If you'd like to try some of these principles out on yourself, the following techniques will help you get started.

1. Foot stretch

Sit on a couch or chair and put one of your feet on top of your opposite thigh, so you can hold your foot with both hands. Working from the heel to the base of the toes with your thumbs, gently spread the tissue by pushing your thumbs away from one another. Then compress the tissue by pushing your thumbs towards each other. With your knuckles, knead your foot, starting at the heel, moving to the toes. Warm up your toes by spreading them apart then squeezing them together, finishing by rotating each toe lightly.

2. Head massage

Sit comfortably and put your hands in front of your face. Press the index, middle and ring fingers of each hand just above your eyebrows. Still pressing, move them up your forehead, to the top of your head, then carry on moving them down the back of your head and release. Repeat 10 times.

> To keep the body in good health is a duty, otherwise we shall not be able to keep the mind strong and clear.

Buddha

CASE STUDY

Balance is all – Krip Rojanastien and Chiva-Som International Health Resorts

Krip Rojanastien is one of the guiding lights at the heart of the Thai wellness industry. As Chairman and CEO of one of the world's most iconic luxury wellness destinations, he helps guests (including famous names like Serena Williams, Hugh Grant and Kate Moss) destress, rejuvenate and find optimal wellbeing.

Chiva-Som, meaning haven of life, is tucked away in 7 acres of lush tropical gardens in the Thai seaside town of Hua Hin, and regularly voted Best Destination Spa in the World. Khun Krip, whose father, Boonchu Rojanastien, founded the resort nearly 30 years ago, says there's a reason why Thailand is home to some of the top holistic

health and wellness retreats. 'We've used massage and movement for centuries to relax the body and focus the mind. They're a core part of our beliefs and culture, while Buddhism, meditation techniques, healthy eating and calm movement are intertwined with daily life and balanced living. To us, balance is everything and is key to rejuvenating, energising and empowering mind, body and spirit.'

Sanuk is important because, 'while it's often translated as "fun", sanuk is so much more than that. It's about striving for enjoyment in everything we do. It's finding the balance of wellbeing in mind, body and spirit, in a sustainable and enjoyable way. It's finding joy in healthy habits and longevity.'

Never has this been more important than in a post-pandemic world: 'Health is by far our most important asset. We must take care of ourselves to live life to its full potential and enjoy all it has to offer.'

Chiva-Som offers online treatments and programmes, but we can all tap into the resort's wellness philosophy by simply finding what brings us joy, says Krip. 'My father's motto was: "Above all, enjoy your life". Choose activities that are good for the spirit, as well as the mind and body. Joy can come in all forms. Don't seek quick fixes or gruelling programmes that you can't maintain but focus on the key elements you can change and incorporate into your day. Step by step, you'll see these habits evolve and grow to create the optimal you.'

Alongside a healthy lifestyle comes the power of community. 'One vitally important part of wellbeing is a sense of community and being part of one. Our relationships and connections to others and our environments are key; spending quality time with friends, family and loved ones is vital to increasing our wellbeing and long-term happiness.'

Friends, family and loved ones … Until we all get the opportunity to spend time at Chiva-Som, what could be more sanuk than that?

The power of a power nap

While massage is the cornerstone of holistic wellbeing in Thailand, there are other concepts that help Thais maintain a sense of sanuk and we'll take a look at a few of them throughout the rest of this chapter. First, Thais know the restorative benefits of a nap. They can fall asleep anywhere, any time. Like most of their tropical neighbours, and their siesta-loving cousins on the continent, they're partial to a mid-afternoon snooze to avoid the intense midday heat. In fact, Sit only has to see a hammock swinging from a tree for his eyes to start drifting shut … There's no stigma associated with sleeping in public. Walking around the city streets, you'll spot tuk-tuk drivers asleep on the back seats of their vehicles, or stallholders dozing precariously on their stools between customers.

It's something we could all benefit from, and Google, NASA and Nike are just a few of the companies who have introduced sleep pods for employees. Far from being a sign of laziness, a nap could help the brain stay healthy, according to some research, equivalent to delaying ageing by between three and six years. Just keep it to less than half an hour.

Healing nature

Thailand is blessed with mind-blowing natural beauty, but wherever you are, you can get health benefits by simply going outside. Being in nature, exercise, daylight and fresh air can have a huge effect on your mood. What's that you say? It's blowing a gale and pouring with rain? Well, amazingly, the power of nature is so strong that you may not even have to leave the house. One study by Dacher Keltner at UC Berkeley found that simply watching a short clip of a nature show leads to significant increases in positive emotions, including

awe, contentedness, joy and amusement. Sanuk win! Feelings of nervousness, anxiety and fear also decreased at the same time. And if you do make it out of the door, time spent in nature sparks a series of happy reactions in our bodies, reducing cortisol (stress) levels, increasing levels of serotonin (the happiness hormone) and even causing us to produce the love hormone, oxytocin (which is great if you're feeling lonely).

Three natural mood boosters

1.

Sun – Just 20 minutes per day in the sunshine can improve your mood and quality of sleep. It's mostly down to the happy hormones which nature helps us produce – and the negative ones it reduces.

2.

Sea – Being near blue spaces and the sight and sounds of water, such as crashing waves, can act as a mental reset and help us gain a sense of perspective on our troubles. The coast brings the most pronounced benefits, but being near any water – lakes, canals, rivers and ponds – can provide a mood boost.

3.

Parks – Even a 15-minute stroll in an urban park provides physical and psychological benefits, including a lowered heart rate and reduced stress.

Find your fitness tribe

When it comes to exercise, the Thai love of community can be seen in the communal outdoor activity areas in each village, where locals of all ages gather for sanuk socialising while getting fit. Whether it's pedalling on an exercise bike or working out on the rowing machine, it's a chance for them to catch up on local news while improving their health.

On the holiday islands, the spirit of sanuk is strong. Every backpacker and tourist soon learns that if they find themselves on a Thai beach at around 5.30pm, just as the weather starts to cool down, they'll see locals arriving with a football for a kickaround. Tourists are welcome to join in, and all different nationalities playing on the sand is a very sanuk way for everyone to come together at the end of a lazy day. It's not taken too seriously, and anyone hogging the ball Ronaldo-style will be swiftly taken down. And there's no better way to cool off than by running into the sea afterwards.

This collective approach is crucial in keeping things fun. Fitness groups give a feeling of belonging and a hefty shot of motivation. It's about being part of something bigger: a community. From a gym buddy who makes a workout session more sociable to the upbeat group dynamic of a local organised 5k weekend park run, getting fit with others boosts motivation and adds a sanuk element to getting healthy.

Muay Thai and Takraw

The martial art Muay Thai (aka Thai boxing) starts almost like a ritualised dance, but when the fighters go on the attack, it's a fast and furious flurry of power and fluidity. Using fists, elbows, legs and knees as weapons, it's a full-body workout that will get you in shape in weeks. Exciting to watch, the fights are sanuk for all.

There's also kick volleyball – sepak takraw (or takrow) – which is played with a hard rattan or plastic ball, with spectacular jumps and flips to kick the ball over the net. Officially, it's played between two teams on a court, but you'll often see a couple of young Thai men having a kickabout with one another as a sanuk way to unwind at the end of the day.

Healing and medicinal herbs

Thai herbalism has been passed down through generations, meaning that as well as being part of their daily diets, herbs are used by Thai people as much for wellbeing as flavour. Whether it's anti-inflammatory turmeric, lemongrass to aid digestion or holy basil to reduce stress and anxiety, their health benefits are now being recognised by modern science.

The Thai term for herb, samunprai, is used for any plant that can be used for health or medicinal purposes – and with an astonishing 2187 plant species reported as medicinal in Thailand, it's big business, too. The Thai herbal medicinal section was valued at 52 billion baht (£1.18 billion) in 2022, and their government is keen to promote their use in public health services. Many Thais use traditional remedies alongside other medicine.

Interestingly, Thailand became the first country in Asia to decriminalise cannabis after it delisted the marijuana plant as a narcotic in 2022.

How to make a Thai herbal compress

Thai herbal compress therapy, Luk Pra Kob, is an ancient healing technique that combines traditional Thai massage with hot herbal compresses. Filled with a blend of aromatic herbs, the compresses are steamed and then gently applied to the body to help relieve muscle tension, improve circulation and promote relaxation.

In addition to promoting deep relaxation, the Thai herbal compress helps relieve stress, improves circulation, stimulates the internal organs and is great for alleviating pain and providing relief to stiff or sore muscles. Based on Ayurvedic and traditional Chinese medicine, herbal compresses are an ancient practice that has been in use for thousands of years in monasteries and temples. A soft cloth ball that is filled with various herbs, the compress can either be used as part of a massage or pressed against skin after a massage for further relaxation. As the moist heat makes its way down through the body, it helps to melt away any tension and soreness while skin absorbs the herbal blend.

The wellness therapists at Bangkok's wellness and medical spa RAKxa share an easy DIY recipe for creating your own Thai herbal compress.

Ingredients
200g dry rice (white or brown)
1 tbsp turmeric powder
1 tbsp cinnamon
1⅓ cup sliced ginger
Unbleached muslin cloth
Yarn or thread

Method

1. Place the rice and the spices in a bowl and mix well.

2. Place the mixture into the centre of your cloth, bringing all the edges up and over the herbs to make a firm, round ball.

3. Tie the top close to the mixture with the yarn or thread to create a handle. Keep the herbal compress ball tight, so that it won't become loose when in use.

4. Place in a microwave for 90 seconds.

Prior to application, check the temperature of the herbal compress ball on the inner forearm. Once the temperature is to your liking, firmly place the herbal compress ball on the required area for 15–30 minutes. Use up to five times.

Spirituality

In Thailand, a predominantly Buddhist country, you're never far from one of the 40,000 temples which grace the landscape with a gleaming golden Buddha or silver spire gracefully reaching into the sky. For Thai people, they play a crucial role in sanuk celebrations and are at the centre of most of their festivals. Temples have an important role in Thai everyday life, too, as people go to pray for good health, good fortune and wealth, seek life advice from monks or simply take the opportunity for some quiet meditation.

On my visits to the temples, I always walk away feeling calmer, the tranquil environment conveying such a sense of serenity. Even if you don't have the opportunity of finding a temple to go to, you can get the same benefit by seeking out peaceful places where you can truly relax and calm your racing thoughts. It could be a park bench, a library or simply a meditative stroll around the neighbourhood where you really notice what's around you; the important thing is to give yourself space to just be …

For me, one of the best times to do this is early morning before the bustle of the day begins. In Thailand, monks wake at 4am, and after meditation and chanting, walk barefoot around the neighbourhood, while the local people 'make merit', to increase their chance of happiness in this and future lives, by offering them food. I'm not advocating such a crack-of-dawn start, but embracing the day by taking the opportunity to sit in quiet contemplation before your daily tasks kick in means you can boost your chances of sanuk by cultivating a sense of wellbeing and inner peace.

The importance of slowing down

Life moves so fast now that days, weeks and months can pass in a blur as we try to keep up with everything. It can leave us feeling stressed, rushed and anxious. Measuring our lives in achievements and by how productive we are has become the norm. But if you're going at 100mph, it's hard to have sanuk. The heat means that Thailand moves to its own slower rhythm, with even city workers walking at an unhurried pace compared to most Westerners.

With no rush, or sense of urgency, I soon got used to the fact that 'Thai time' is flexible. And slowing down comes with many benefits. It's a more mindful way of living that allows you to appreciate all the good things that are going on in your daily life. It's only by slowing down and switching out of autopilot that we can really take things in. When we're rushing around from place to place or can't keep up with all our thoughts and mental to-do lists, we're not connected.

Although sanuk is a social concept, the meaning is personal, too. We must find joy and happiness within ourselves, as well as with other people. With modern life giving rise to increased problems with anxiety, depression, disordered eating and self-esteem issues, we need to embrace sanuk as a way of reclaiming a positive mental attitude and inner contentment. The Land of Smiles has much to teach us here. In Thailand, Buddhism is a key part of everyday life and synonymous with tranquillity and peace of mind. Central to Buddhism is the

There is no other happiness but peace.

Thai proverb

practice of meditation, which helps to reduce anxiety, improve focus and promote overall wellness. This Eastern discipline helps to ease muscle tension and is proven to reduce anxiety, blood pressure and heart rate (see p. 165 for a simple mindfulness technique you can do anywhere). If you find it hard to keep focus, guided meditation led by a teacher, whether in person or via audio or video, can be useful; I like the Headspace app (see Resources, p. 264), where co-founder and former Buddhist monk Andy Puddicombe offers a range of exercises, but you might want to find a local meditation class and meet like-minded people for an extra shot of sanuk.

Live better, longer

People are living longer in the 21st century, and Thailand is at the forefront of this trend, with the number of centenarians per 100,000 people exceeding that of the developed West:

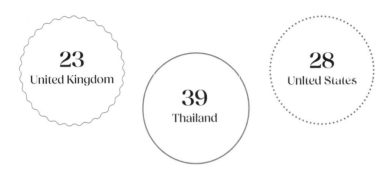

While genetics play a role in longer life, unsurprisingly, good habits also matter. Studies show links between longevity and not just exercise, but social activities. So those social bonds so key to sanuk also help us live better, as well as longer.

An ongoing study by Northwestern Medicine into the secrets of so-called 'super-agers' (those who live beyond 80 with cognitive abilities on par with those up to 30 years younger) has reported they have more warm, trusting, high-quality relationships with other people. Optimism, another key driver of sanuk, matters, too, with a link between that and longer lifespans among women. Yet another reason to look on the bright side of life!

9.

Get the Sanuk Look

– Satai Sanuk

Home is where the heart is. Not where it once was.

Thai proverb

Thai people use the spirit of sanuk to decorate and adorn their homes and places of work, and as a visual reminder of their faith and beliefs, which play a big part in making them happy. Sanuk style is also about visual stimulation, decorations and objects that inspire and promote happiness: a plain pack of tissues will be kept in an ornate silver box, an elaborately patterned Thai silk sarong will hang on the wall, beautifully carved teak furniture is a work of art, garlands of flowers are draped from car mirrors to protect the occupants of the vehicles. Throughout the home and the spaces Thai people inhabit, bold, bright colours spark joy and optimism.

Thailand's location at the crossroads of Southeast Asia has made it a melting pot of different influences and its people love to take and adapt the best of other cultures. So whether it's weaving through traffic on an adrenaline-charged taxi ride in a kitsch three-wheeled tuk-tuk rickshaw complete with Buddha charms, pumping music and flashing disco lights, appeasing the spirit world with a can of Fanta or tying a brightly coloured cloth as a sign of respect around an ancient tree, they bring a lightness and spirituality to their way of living.

In the heart of the home are mementoes of happy, sanuk times, as well as references to their faith; my in-laws are among the small number of Catholics in the country, and family photos of weddings and graduation ceremonies share shelf space with images of Jesus and the Thai royal family, while in our UK home, Sit's Buddhist faith means that images and statues of Buddha gaze down benevolently on us in every room, sending a powerful message of serenity.

Whether traditional or modern, the common theme running through Thai homes is the use of natural materials and bringing elements of the outdoors in. In this chapter, I'll show how you can create a joyful environment and cultivate a feeling of sanuk in your own home and style.

Sanuk your space

Like everything in their culture, Thai people take a holistic approach to design in the home, the feel and aroma of a room being just as important as the appearance. Here are a few key principles to bear in mind to create a sanuk-enhancing atmosphere.

Encourage flow

With an emphasis on harmony and balance, natural light and open spaces are important. Large windows and doors allow light to flood in, while uncluttered living areas bring about a feeling of airiness and flow. This positive energy flow helps create a sense of spaciousness and joy – the ideal arena for sanuk entertaining.

Natural materials

The Thai love of nature is reflected in the use of materials such as wood and stone. Alongside silk, cotton and linen, you'll find skilfully carved wooden panels, screens, doors and chairs made from beautiful teak, with light and flexible bamboo and rattan used for everything from furniture to baskets. Incorporate natural and woven fabrics into your interior for a sense of calm.

Decoration inspiration

Including Thai art in your home adds a joyful touch. Look for paintings, sculptures and ceramics that feature elephant carvings or scenes from traditional Thai life. Gold or silver vessels give a lush touch, alongside vases, bowls and figurines decorated with intricate designs. Textures are key, added with the use of different materials, such as textile wall hangings and cushions.

Play with colour

Red, gold and green are considered auspicious: red for good luck and prosperity; gold for wealth and status; green for nature, balance and harmony. Use these colours to create vibrant features and contrasts, bringing a sense of adventure to your living space. Choose richly coloured fabrics for anything from a silk runner along the edge of a bed to decorative cushions on chairs.

Use patterns

Thai textiles often feature traditional motifs, such as lotus flowers and paisley. Look for fabrics and accessories that incorporate these designs to add a pop of colour and cultural references to your home. In modern Thai homes, these images can be woven in with clean lines and contemporary elements.

Add aroma

Ramp up the Asian factor by creating an entire sensory experience and bring tropical fragrance to rooms using scented candles or oils. Look for authentic-smelling candles and incense such as lotus, lemongrass, sandalwood, ylang-ylang, jasmine, patchouli, sage and rose – even lime and mango.

Bring the outside in

Thais love to enjoy their sanuk outdoors, so they treat the fronts of their homes as an extra room. A large table outside to gather with friends and family on warm evenings is essential for their sanuk. If there's space, an area is left open to allow a tree to grow. Often flowering or

scented, it provides delicious fragrance, as well as shade in the heat of the day. In less tropical climes, we can all add some greenery to an indoor living space – look for plants such as orchids, bamboo and palms.

Hang a hammock

There's not a tree in Thailand which hasn't been assessed to see if it might be close enough to its neighbour for a hammock to be slung between them. Hammocks are very sanuk – they're all about chilling out, with a frisson of fun, as there's always the risk of toppling out and falling flat on your face.

Incorporate elephants

A national symbol, elephants have an important place in the country's culture and identity dating back centuries. In 1817, the official flag of Thailand, then known as Siam, was a white elephant in the middle of a scarlet background. Today, the elephant is found on everything from clothes to beer labels.

Try a triangular cushion

There's nothing more sanuk for Thai people; time spent relaxing with others is time well spent, and brightly coloured and embroidered Thai floor cushions make a fabulously comfortable bed on which to do so. A centuries-old traditional handicraft that first appeared in northern Thailand, these triangular pillow and mattress combos have a multitude of uses. They're found in many homes, while any tourist who's ever stopped for a beer in a Thai beach bar will have lounged on one. They were a revelation when I first spotted them in Bangkok 30 years ago, but these days they're easy to find.

The Little Book of Sanuk

Nine ways to get the sanuk look

1.
Bold colours

2.
Natural materials

3.
Woven fabrics

4.
Bamboo baskets

5.
Silver serving bowls

6.
Decorative lamps

7.
Bright paintings

8.
Outdoor lights

9.
Tropical plants

Your lucky Thai colour

Thai people have colours assigned for every day, and the day you were born is your lucky colour. Traditionally, people would choose this for their clothes, but there's nothing stopping you from using it in your home, too.

Sunday = red

Monday = yellow

Tuesday = pink

Wednesday = green

Thursday = orange

Friday = light blue

Saturday = violet

CASE STUDY

Comfort in the everyday – Teerachai Suppameteekulwat and Qualy

With a concept of creativity, happiness and sustainability, Thai decor brand Qualy bring a sense of playfulness to the home. Its quirky yet functional products are guaranteed to put a smile on people's faces. Co-founder and design director Toorachai Suppameteekulwat says, 'We believe in the power of design to enhance a better life and better world'.

Their cute and clever designs often feature animals and nature with fun hidden gimmicks to bring sanuk style to the home. 'Key elements of Thai design are positivity and a sense of humour, along with harmony, flexibility and humility,' says Teerachai. 'For us, the design must be useful, and resolve a problem or create something better. Happiness and wellbeing can come from making life simpler or less confusing. Design can assist by creating items to provide comfort in the everyday.'

Channelling the hopeful spirit of sanuk, Qualy seek to make a difference to the future of the planet, with sustainability and the circular economy at the heart of their work. 'Our philosophy is to respect our planet and, in the meantime, improve people's lives. Although we're in the midst of an environmental crisis, we are optimistic; it's not too late if we all make a change together. If the best time to plant a tree was 20 years ago, the second-best time is now.'

To be inspired by Thai design for our own homes, take a relaxed approach, says Teerachai. 'Keeping things simple and functional in the home will bring sanuk. Compromise, be empathetic and don't worry about being flawless, because all the rules are flexible.'

Flexible rules? The most sanuk kind!

Spirituality in the home

Spirituality and spiritual symbols play an important role in representing Thailand's culture and heritage. You will see them everywhere, from public places to private homes, and they act as signposts for others about the things which matter to Thai people, telling stories and reflecting their values.

Flowers carry a special meaning within Buddhism, and the lotus flower, a design seen on many artworks and fabrics as well as in temples, is the most sacred. They are particularly symbolic because they generally grow in muddy, shallow water, growing upwards towards the light and warmth to bloom into beautiful flowers. Every day, they are once again submerged into the mud and bloom again the next day. To Buddhists, this natural rebirth is representative of the act of spiritual growth and reaching enlightenment; regardless of who we are, we have the capacity to rise above our challenges and limitations.

Buddhism, which emphasises gentleness and compliance, is important in defining the Thai character. While images and symbols of Buddha are common in Thai homes, it's worth remembering that such images are religious objects to Thais, not merely home decor, so should be treated with respect.

Thai people are superstitious, and alongside Buddhism or Hinduism, they mix in traditional beliefs including ghosts and spirits. Outside many homes are spirit houses called 'San Phra Phum' or shrine of the guardian spirit, which are believed to be dwelling places for the spirits of the deceased. Ranging from small, unassuming wooden structures to beautiful, highly decorated and brightly coloured mini temples, all are garlanded in flowers, and piled with food, fizzy drinks and incense sticks every morning to keep the spirits happy. These offerings can even include cigarettes and bottles of Mekong whisky!

Sanuk dressing

Their easy-going approach to life means that for Thai people, choosing what to wear is generally whatever makes you happy. But while pretty much anything goes, you'll rarely see Thais clad in head-to-toe black. Here are a few ideas for sanuk style.

Natural fabrics

The tropical climate is a good reason for Thais to choose natural, breathable materials like silk and cotton. But whatever the weather, natural fabrics are a great option – durable, environmentally sustainable and naturally hypo-allergenic.

Embrace ease

In city jobs, a uniform or smart work wardrobe gives a sense of pride, but at the end of the day, Thais mark the shift from work mode by changing into the casual, loose-fitting styles which signal it's time to relax. Switch off from your day job and get a healthy work/life balance by doing the same.

Living colour

As in the home, vibrant colours and bold patterns reflect Thai people's love of beauty and creativity. Some research also shows that wearing brightly coloured clothes can boost mood. Fashion experts have dubbed the trend 'dopamine dressing', because of the feelgood effect it brings. Almost everyone in Thailand owns a bright, flowery shirt, if only to wear for the Songkran festival celebrations (see pp. 14–19). Sanuk style for all generations!

Playful prints

Many Thai teens and young women love a cute, cartoony look and worship at the altar of Hello Kitty. For adults, the light and baggy 'elephant pants' (so called as they're usually printed with a colourful elephant design) have moved from backpackers' beach wardrobe to citywear for visitors. Fun, comfortable and useful to keep the sun and insects off your legs, they're a sanuk solution to tropical living.

Flip-flop fun

The Thai custom of removing your shoes when you enter someone's home, temples and even some shops and restaurants, means people need footwear that's easy to slip on and off. Anything with laces is way too much hassle, so cheap flip-flops are often the footwear of choice. Plus, there can be sanuk at the end of the night, as everyone tries to find their matching pair among the mound of similar-looking rubber sandals piled outside the entrance.

The Little Book of Sanuk

A creative nation

Thailand is a country of creators, makers and artists. From silver jewellery and lacquerware to ceramics, silks, mulberry paper and puppets, their handmade crafts are famous throughout the world.

We may never reach the Thais' level of skill, but crafting is a nice way of getting a sense of sanuk for yourself and your home. Craft is proven to benefit mental wellbeing; aside from the meditative quality of repetition, doing something which requires focus and attention can provide healthy distraction from any stresses.

Get crafting

Check out if there are any craft clubs in your area. From knitting, embroidery and crochet to card-making workshops and pottery, you'll get to meet artistic souls sharing their skills, and walk away with your own unique handmade creation.

Phone a friend. Add to your crafting sanuk by getting a like-minded pal to come, too. You can share your skill-learning journey, have fun together and keep each other motivated.

Can't decide on a craft? If you haven't done anything creative since school, think about what you enjoyed back then. Chances are it will still bring you sanuk. Or look on YouTube for inspiration. Video tutorials are a great place to start; and even if you don't try them, those 'weird-but-cool-crafts' videos are sanuk viewing.

Joy through creativity – Ploenchan 'Mook' Vinyaratn, textile artist and designer

Mook is a textile artist with a storied background in designing handwoven rugs and hand-embroidered cushion covers which are fixtures at five-star resorts throughout Thailand and the Asia Pacific region. From her early career helping to teach villagers and hill tribes how to use modern weaving techniques to create contemporary designs, she launched her award-winning textile company, Beyond Living, in 2003. Blending local raw materials with innovative resources and techniques, her work has led to collaborations with luxury fashion houses and helped usher in an exciting new era of Thai textiles.

For Mook, sanuk embodies the joy of creativity. 'It's crafting pieces that captivate the eyes and touch the soul. It's infusing my creations with a sense of playfulness, vibrant colours, deeper meanings and the rich textures inspired by Thai traditions.'

Thailand's handmade local arts and crafts act as an inspiration for an artist who looks to the past and puts a modern-day spin on it. 'As tangible artifacts of our cultural identity, their positive energy and intricate patterns express the joy that the skilled artisans experience in creating their work,' Mook says. 'Their happy spirit shines through in their creations.'

Continuing the sustainable practices of the past, the Bangkok designer works with upcycled and repurposed materials. She creates environmental talking points with stunning sculptures and installations made from rubbish, old fishing nets and marine waste. One of her most powerful artworks is the 40-metre-long mixed media homage to life

along the river, which bends and curves along the ceiling of a Louis Vuitton store in Bangkok.

In the home, Mook suggests using Thai living inspiration to create a sanuk space to bring people together using colourful triangular cushions arranged in a conversation circle.

'The charm of Thai design is that functional items can be more than just utilities; they become storytellers,' she says. 'By taking a modest or "boring" piece of furniture, such as a cushion, and giving it a place in your home you can create an area that allows you to connect with family and friends. You'll often see this on Thai beaches: friends sitting on woven mats, leaning on triangle pillows with their shoes off, watching a fire-dance show, sipping nectar from a coconut that was just hacked open. It's a feeling of bliss. Recreate the mood by setting up a low table surrounded by triangle cushions so that you can almost imagine – with the lights dimmed low – the sound of softly crashing waves in the distance.'

While it may require some creativity to conjure up this vision on a cold winter's night, imagination is a powerful tool. With sanuk benefits guaranteed, what better reason for indulging in such a fantasy could there be?

10.

Let's Eat Together

– Gin Kao Gan

Eating by oneself
brings no joy.
A delicacy should not
be eaten alone.

Buddha

Though my Thai is limited, I always know when my Thai friends and family are discussing our next meal. The conversation gets louder and more animated as everyone chips in with suggestions, and there's lots of laughter among the chatter. On the sanuk scale, it's a 10.

Thai people *love* their food, and this final chapter is perhaps most key to understanding sanuk. Food is connected to so many of the topics I've explored so far in the context of achieving sanuk: from cooking for loved ones to sharing food with communities and having large spaces to eat in our homes, the Thai ethos of serving and eating food and the spirit of sanuk are closely intertwined, with social bonds at their very heart. Thai people eat well – and often. Food is not an enemy to be avoided but a good excuse to spend time with friends, family and co-workers. It's a profoundly social urge.

Food is almost always shared. Sharing a meal with loved ones or preparing a special dish for a celebration foster social connections, as well as sparking positive emotions. Because even though it's something we do every day, eating is fundamentally an emotional act, tied to survival, joy, pleasure, connectedness and fun – many of the themes we've explored in this book. And the fact that we do it so often means it offers many opportunities for connection and enjoyment.

Thai people increase their chances of this connection by making it happen whenever they can; they welcome guests into their homes and show their generosity by offering anything they might have. If you do get invited to eat with Thai people – which is almost guaranteed once you meet them – dinner will be a relaxed occasion. Plus, the non-judgemental spirit of sanuk means they're accepting of all shapes and sizes – beacons of body positivity in a critical age. I've never once heard them discuss calories or diets; but neither have I seen them fill their faces until they're too full to move.

They eat delicately but enthusiastically, enjoying each mouthful. This is not only more aesthetically pleasing than seeing people shovelling food down as fast as they can, but is also easier on the digestive system, giving their bodies time to let them know they are already full, so there's less chance of overeating.

Generally speaking, Thai dishes are very quick to prepare and cook and are served in smaller portions. I'll never forget the look on Sit's face when we first visited my sister's house in Suffolk. She was making a massive casserole and put it on to slow cook for hours while we took the dogs for a long walk. When it was served, while delicious, the huge portion, along with a football-sized baked potato was just too much for Sit, who politely cleared his plate, but left the table groaning.

A communal experience

Thai people don't just love to eat – they love to eat together and to include everyone. Hospitality and generosity are part of their nature, and an important feature of a sanuk experience is sharing food. But because sharing a delicious and easy-to-prepare meal with family, friends and community is part of daily life, Thai people just don't stress about it.

Having said that, not for them are the metallic ping of the microwave and a ready meal on their laps in front of the TV. Meal planning can go on for hours, as what dishes to eat, where to buy them and the best food stall for each ingredient are analysed at length.

With one survey finding that nearly 8 in 10 Brits feel the pressure to make sure their guests are having a good time when they host, and 4 in 10 are glad when it's all over, taking a more sanuk approach to entertaining makes life easier all round. Thais know that peak sanuk is

The Little Book of Sanuk

to be found in the company and sustenance, not in perfectly assembled canapes or an expensive bottle of wine. So why not relax and enjoy …

Thai cuisine is renowned for its vibrant flavours, and the enjoyment of food is considered an essential part of the sanuk experience. Any social gathering, whether it's at the local temple or someone's house, will start at the crack of dawn with the first to rise heading off to market to pick up fresh, locally sourced ingredients. As guests start arriving, everyone will help with preparation, chatting as they chop veg and pummel spices. Soon, delicious smelling curries and soups will be bubbling away. Street food is so good, and so freely available, that there's no shame in grabbing a freshly made stir-fry or noodle dish as a takeaway to add to the spread. In fact, quite the opposite – a trip to the market food stall is a sanuk experience all of its own, and sometimes home kitchens are barely used.

As well as the social aspect of communal eating, Thais have a healthy appreciation for the food they eat, and for those who provide it. With a belief that wasting food brings bad luck, they will not leave it unfinished on their plates unless it's not edible. The plate should be clean of all food, especially rice, to show respect to the rice farmer.

SANUK TIP

Take a break from restaurant chains and embrace street-food culture. Most town centres now have markets with authentic, freshly made dishes from around the globe.

Retail therapy of the most sanuk kind!

Sanuk street markets

Thai people love to shop, and Bangkok is essentially one giant market. And while the nation has embraced giant shopping malls as the perfect way to combine their favourite pastime and cool off in free air-con, street markets remain at the heart of their social life. In most markets you'll find stalls selling fried insects, such as silkworms and grasshoppers and even scorpions. They're not something I've been adventurous enough to try, but locals love them – they're low in calories, high in protein, cheap and nutritious and far healthier than a bag of crisps. Eating them also has historical roots: a worm called the stem borer was one of King Rama V's favourite snacks in the nineteenth century. Food stalls command particular loyalty; every Thai person has their go-to favourites.

I love street shopping and these are three of the best markets for a sanuk time:

1. Maeklong railway market

What do you do when a railway track is built right through a busy market? In Thailand, you simply work around it … Eight times a day, on hearing the warning clang, traders speedily clear their stalls off the line, wait for the train to pass through, then put them back, as if nothing happened. Also known as Siang Tai (life-risking) market or Hoop Rom (umbrella/parasol-closing) market, it is situated 80km southwest of Bangkok.

2. Floating markets

An ancient way of shopping on Bangkok's rivers, now mainly for tourists, this is still a stunning sight. Damnoen Saduak is the most photogenic – huge, lively, full of boats selling food and fruits and the setting for a chaotic chase scene in the James Bond movie *The Man with the Golden Gun*. You can find it 100km southwest of Bangkok.

3. Chatuchak weekend market

This is one for hardcore shoppers. Sprawling across 35 acres, with 15,000 stalls and 200,000 visitors a day, you can grab a free map and be prepared to haggle over clothes, accessories, handicrafts, furniture, plants, art, books, antiques and so much more … It's open every Friday night, Saturday and Sunday and is located in northern Bangkok (Skytrain to Mo Chit Station).

Feast like a Thai

It's better to have many guests at the table rather than just one or two. In fact, some Thais believe that eating alone is bad luck. When Thai people gather for a celebration a communal table for social gatherings will feature some, or all, of these:

- A centrepiece of fresh fish, served with sriracha, the eye-watering chilli sauce they love.
- Snacks and sides, such as crispy spring rolls, chicken satay and sesame prawn toast.
- A huge pot of kai palo – a non-spicy, sweet-and-savoury stew made with pork, tofu and egg, ostensibly for kids, but like catnip to adults.
- Ha mok pla – steamed fish cake made with red curry paste and coconut cream, served in a cup of banana leaves.
- Pla tod kamin – deep-fried fish with garlic and turmeric.
- Seafood tom yum – with fresh prawns and squid.
- Beef and potato massaman curry.
- Kao ka moo – slow-braised pork leg, a street-food favourite.
- Som tam – green papaya salad with dried shrimp and peanuts.
- Knom jim – spicy fresh fish served in a soup with white noodles (aka Thai spaghetti).
- Yum mama – noodles tossed with spicy dressing.
- For dessert, sticky rice with sweet milk and sliced mango; or durian, when in season – it's a very sanuk fruit, as it smells like vomit, but tastes delicious, so is always served with a big smile.

Eating out

Food forms a central part of any Thai social occasion – in fact, it often becomes *the* social occasion, or reason to celebrate. When Thais go to restaurants, the social vibe continues. Remember that episode of the TV show *Friends* where Matt Le Blanc's character was horrified at a dinner date stealing a couple of chips off his plate? ('Joey doesn't share food!') Thai dining is his basic nightmare, but for the rest of us, it's a sanuk-filled delight.

Rather than a starter followed by the main course and dessert, with each person ordering only for themselves, in Thailand, there is no such thing as a starter or any dish that belongs only to one person. In restaurants, everything is ordered for sharing, and when one dish turns out to be particularly delicious and disappears fast, it is re-ordered so everyone gets the chance to try it. Usually, the most senior member of the family or the one who foots the bill will do the ordering, as everyone calls out favourite dishes. With plain rice as the base, there will be at least one dish per person. The central feature of a meal is usually fish, chicken or pork, with curries, spicy salads, soups and stir-fries to add a range of tastes and textures.

> A cheerful heart
> is good medicine.
> But not on an empty stomach.
>
> Thai proverb

Sharing gives everyone a chance to try different foods and is an ideal way to introduce youngsters to new flavours. There's nothing sanuk about mealtime battles, and this way of dining helps to create healthier eating habits for the future.

Everything tends to arrive at the same time and dishes are usually placed in the middle of the table to be shared and enjoyed together. Guests and the elderly are served first; children know to wait their turn.

SANUK TIP
Try to eat with others as often as possible. Communal eating is associated with feelings of happiness, life satisfaction, community involvement and strong social bonds – all key elements for positive emotional health.

How to create a sanuk spread at home

Sharing a delicious and easy to prepare meal with your family, friends and community is peak sanuk. Here are some easy ways to get sanuk vibes when eating in your own home.

- Invite friends or neighbours over; if you're on a tight budget, do a pot-luck dinner, where everyone brings a different element of the meal.
- Serve everything in communal bowls. Simple one-pot meals like soups and stews are easy to prepare; or in the summer, go for giant salads bursting with healthy, vibrant veg.
- If the weather allows, eat outside. Warm evenings are perfect for setting up a spread outdoors and means less clearing up afterwards.
- Set a happy table. Bring out your most colourful crockery and table decorations. If you're outdoors, string up some fairy lights or light candles.
- Don't overthink it. Eating communally is in our genes – if our ancestors could rustle up a spread, so can we!
- If you do just one thing … eat at the table: it's easier to chat when you're facing each other and it helps you to focus on your meal. But if your table is too small … well, we used to have picnics on the living-room floor.

The language of food

GIN KHAO YANG – Have you eaten yet? The warmest greeting in Thai culture, it's used like 'how are you?'

GIN KAO – Dinnertime (literally, 'eat rice')

HEW – Hungry

PET – Spicy

MAI PET – Not spicy

AROI – Delicious

AROI MAK MAR – Very delicious

MAI SAI GATIAM – Don't add garlic

MAI SAI NAM TAN – Don't add sugar

GIN JAY/JAY – Vegan

MANG SA WIRAT – No meat (but may include eggs, as well as fish and oyster sauce)

IM LAU – Full up (refers to being replete with food; my friend Gary once said this jokingly as people tried to enter a packed Bangkok lift, only to be met with polite bewilderment)

Cooking the sanuk way

There is a huge disconnect in our modern-day relationship with food, as evidenced by the fact that the weight-loss industry was worth an incredible U$224.27 billion [£181.26 billion] in 2021 (and expected to surpass $405.4 billion [£327.65 billion] by 2030), while obesity is now recognised as one of the most important public-health problems facing the world today.

The first rule of food sanuk is that there are no rules. Fancy having last night's leftovers for breakfast? Go for it. Thai people don't really have breakfast foods as such, they normally eat their beloved rice and noodles. I've been known to start my Bangkok day with freshly made pha tong ko – deliciously moreish finger doughnuts – dunked into Nom Yen (Thai pink milk). Not the healthiest of morning meals, but no judgement was made – and it was balanced out by the fresh food I ate the rest of the day. And that balance is key: eating what you actually want can mean you feel more satisfied with your meal, whereas if you deny yourself, you might go on to have unhealthy snacks anyway. Depriving yourself of what you really want can lead to obsessive behaviour and poor food choices – the very opposite of the joy that food should bring.

Taking a more sanuk approach to our diets means tuning into what our bodies are telling us – eating when we're hungry and stopping when we feel full. And by focusing on the pleasure that food brings we can help make that shift. The sight and aroma of food can bring us almost as much pleasure as the food itself, so whether it's a colourful red, green or yellow curry, or a mound of stir-fried green, leafy vegetables, or the delicious smell of crushed garlic frying in a wok, Thai mealtimes are a sanuk, sensory overload.

Pretty plates

Presentation is a key part of Thai food culture, and top chefs love to create delicate and intricate carvings from fruits and vegetables. Known as kae sa luk, this is an unmistakably Thai tradition that's as beautiful as it is delicious. Fruit and vegetable carving was originally used to decorate the tables of the royal family, but now you can see tomatoes transformed into roses, cucumbers into flower petals or an apple turned into a swan at celebratory dinners and in upmarket Thai hotels and resorts. But wherever you are, presentation is always important, and whether it's a street-food restaurant or a hotel, your meal is likely to be served with pretty decorations.

Sanuk ingredients

Go into any Thai kitchen and I can guarantee you will spot these!

RICE – Whether it's long-grain, jasmine or sticky, rice is a Thai staple. Every family has a rice cooker turned on 24/7 to ensure hot, freshly cooked rice is always available for sanuk snacking.

FISH SAUCE – This salty seasoning, usually made from anchovies, smells disgusting, but used sparingly as a dipping sauce with garlic, chillies, sugar and lime juice, gives food a sanuk kick.

OYSTER SAUCE AND SRIRACHA SAUCE – These give savoury dishes a boost and help add umami, complexity and depth to meat and vegetable stir-fries.

SOY SAUCE – Light and dark, both are added liberally to stir-fries, used to marinate meat and fish or served on the side.

GALANGAL – A root used in tom yum and tom kha soups for flavour, aka Thai ginger, but don't make the mistake of trying to eat it.

EGGS – Boiled, fried or made into a vegetable omelette with the tender green tips of the shrub cha-om, eggs are a cheap and sanuk way of bulking out a meal and adding protein; few dishes aren't improved by their addition.

SUGAR – Sweet-toothed Thais add this to everything from papaya salads to noodle soup.

Sit's simple, sanuk-inspired recipes

There are so many delicious Thai dishes, but these classics are quick and easy crowd-pleasers to make at home for guests.

Chicken Satay Sticks

Thai people love grabbing these as a quick on-the-move snack as they shop in markets.

Serves 4

Ingredients

450g boneless, skinless chicken thighs, cut into strips

Chicken marinade	*Satay peanut sauce for dipping*
5 garlic cloves	100g ground peanuts
Garlic pepper, to taste	2 tbsp peanut butter
3 tbsp fish sauce	1 tbsp massaman curry paste
1 tbsp soy sauce	400ml coconut milk
1 tsp ground turmeric	2 tbsp light soy sauce
2 tsp ground coriander	1 tbsp fish sauce
2 tbsp liquid honey	1 tbsp brown sugar
2 tbsp vegetable oil	
100ml coconut milk	

1. Whizz all the marinade ingredients together in a food processor to create a richly flavoured paste. Pour three quarters of the paste over the chicken and stir well. Cover and put in the refrigerator to marinate for an hour.

2. While the chicken is marinating, place 12–15 wooden satay sticks in your sink and cover with water to prevent burning.

3. Skewer the marinated chicken on to the sticks. Place meat near the sharp end, leaving space at the other end so you can pick up the stick to turn it.

4. Place the satays under a hot grill. Turn them over after 5 minutes and bast with the remaining marinade. Continue to cook, turning occasionally, until the meat is browned with charred edges and opaque inside, and any juices run clear (about 15 minutes).

5. For the dipping sauce, add all the ingredients to a small pan. Heat gently, stirring until the sugar dissolves and the sauce thickens slightly. Transfer to a bowl and allow to cool.

Super-speedy Pad Thai

There's no shame in using ready-made sauces; Thai brands give authentic flavour and save time and effort. Quick to prepare, this can be made with chicken or veg, and you can add chilli flakes at the end to make it as spicy or as mild as you choose. For me, the prawn version ticks all the taste boxes.

Serves 4

Ingredients

250g flat rice noodles
2 tbsp vegetable oil
½ red onion, chopped
150g peeled tiger prawns
3 eggs
2 tbsp fish sauce
100ml Pad Thai seasoning
   [I use Maepranom]
1 tbsp sriracha hot chilli sauce
4 spring onions, sliced
320g vegetable and beansprout
   stir-fry pack

To serve
25g coriander
Chilli flakes (optional)
2 limes, cut into wedges
25g crushed peanuts
Sweet chilli sauce

The Little Book of Sanuk

1. Place the noodles into a large bowl, cover with boiling water and leave until just softened. Drain and rinse under cold water, then drain again.

2. Heat the oil in a wok or large frying pan and fry the chopped onion for 2–3 minutes, until soft and golden, then add the prawns and cook for another 2 minutes, until pink.

3. Add the eggs, quickly stirring until they have scrambled. Add the noodles and toss for 2 minutes.

4. Add the fish sauce, and a dash of water.

5. Add the Pad Thai seasoning, sriracha sauce, half of the sliced spring onions and the stir-fry pack. Stir over a hot heat for 30 seconds.

6. Cook for a few minutes, until everything is heated through.

7. Pile into a large dish, scatter with coriander and the remaining spring onions and serve with the chilli flakes (if desired), lime wedges to squeeze over, crushed peanuts on the side and sweet chilli sauce.

Easy ginger drink

Ginger is delicious and a brilliant anti-inflammatory. Once a week, Sit boils up a pan of this, which we cool and keep in the fridge to use as a base for vegetable smoothies. It's super sweet on its own, so I add it to the Nutribullet with whatever we have in the salad drawer – spinach, carrot, celery, cucumber, beetroot, apple – and I throw in chia seeds, wheatgrass and spirulina powder, too, for a sanuk way to start my day.

Makes 1 litre

Ingredients
1 litre water
300g roughly chopped ginger root
300g dark brown sugar

1. Boil all the ingredients together for 45 minutes, strain into airtight containers, leave to cool and then refrigerate.

SANUK TIP

Sharing a meal can be a special time to connect and catch up. But if you despair of your offspring's fussy eating, it might help to know that children need to be exposed to a new food up to 15 times before they'll accept it.

Conclusion

This book has given you an introduction to sanuk and how you can apply it to all areas of your life. Throughout, I've tried to distil the essence of this concept and provide useful tips, too – no trip to Thailand required. (Although if you are lucky enough to be able to go, you'll now have a deeper understanding of the culture of its kind and fun-loving people.)

By now, you will have gathered that it's almost a rule of living for Thai people that whatever they do, it has to be sanuk. For them, every endeavour has a little bit of fun involved, whether at work, school or home. It's about getting moments of joy into even the most routine, day-to-day situations. When I first mentioned writing a book on sanuk to Thai friends and family, they were excited, but a little confused. Was this really such a novel concept? Surely every culture wanted some fun and playfulness in their lives? That's because the concept of sanuk is so embedded in the Thais' DNA that they don't always notice it. What they do know, however, is that happiness is more about how you look at life than what actually happens.

For me, the beauty of a life filled with sanuk is that it is within the grasp of all of us. It's making the most of every day, without worrying about what the future will bring. It's a way to enjoy the life we have right now, rather than putting things on hold, until a mythical better future. And the benefits are so clear – not just more fun, but better mental health, happier kids, a more fulfilling work life …

Living my best sanuk life!

In times of conflict and anxiety, finding the small things that give us pleasure can help us all to live rich and joyful lives. Embracing the present, enjoying the everyday and finding beauty in what is around us right now, rather than constantly craving more, are the keys to happiness.

Sanuk often entails acts of kindness, sharing laughter and spreading joy – all things which involve others. It comes from our relationships – not just our friends and family, but the community around us.

Adopting sanuk in my everyday has been a life-changer for me, and I hope that after reading this book you will be inspired to embrace it too.

Sanuk mai? Sanuk!

Resources

Wellbeing

Chiva Som, destination spa resort: chivasom.com

RAKxa, integrative wellness: rakxawellness.com

The Cabin Rehab, luxury drug and alcohol addiction treatment centre: thecabinchiangmai.com

The Wildlife Trusts, a federation of UK wildlife conservation charities: wildlifetrusts.org

Relate, the largest provider of relationship support in England and Wales: relate.org.uk

Counselling Thailand, professional counselling services in English and Thai: counsellingthailand.com

Ani Naqvi, executive mentor: ultimateresultsgroup.com

NHS Every Mind Matters, clinical evidence-based and NHS-endorsed resource: nhs.uk/every-mind-matters (Please note that the NHS/ Department of Health and Social Care does not endorse the book's content)

Mind, working to improve the lives of people with mental health problems: mind.org.uk

Shelter, housing charity offering advice and support services for housing issues and homelessness: shelter.org.uk

Headspace app, mindfulness tools: headspace.com

Wellthy Clinic, co founded by Eleonora Sansoni, is a London clinic which works across osteopathy, nutrition and Pilates: wellthyclinic.com

Get involved

Pets as Therapy, a charity that strives to ensure that everyone has access to the companionship of an animal, with visits to care homes, hospitals, hospices, schools and prisons: petsastherapy.org

Good Gym, a community of people who get fit by doing good: goodgym.org

Re-engage, committed to older people being heard, valued and engaged: reengage.org.uk

Sense, disability charity who believe everyone should be able to take part in life, no matter their disability: sense.org.uk

The Silverline, free, confidential 24-hour-a-day telephone service for older people: thesilverline.org.uk (0800 470 8090)

Samaritans, free, confidential 24-hour-a-day listening and support to people in times of need: samaritans.org (116 123)

Volunteering Matters, bringing people together to overcome adversity and some of society's most complex issues through the power of volunteering: volunteeringmatters.org.uk

NHS Blood Donation, become a blood donor: blood.co.uk

The Friendly Bench: active, social hubs where free, community-led activities and events encourage everyone to participate, have fun, feel valued and develop a support network: thefriendlybench.co.uk

Parkrun, free, community 5k event – walk, jog, run, volunteer or spectate: parkrun.org.uk

Mental Health UK, support for people affected by mental-health problems: mentalhealth-uk.org

Books

The Power of Fun: Why Fun is the Key to a Happy and Healthy Life, by Catherine Price (Penguin Random House, 2022)

The Myth of Multitasking: How 'Doing it All' Gets Nothing Done by Dave Crenshaw (Mango Media, 2021)

On Belonging: Finding Connection in an Age of Isolation, by Kim Samuel (Abrams Press, 2022)

10 Keys to Happier Living: A Practical Handbook for Happiness by Vanessa King (Headline Hachette, 2016)

Happiness: Lessons from a New Science, Richard Layard (Penguin, 2005)

Research sources

The Thaiger, English-language news site: thethaiger.com

The Gottman Institute, a research-based approach to relationships: gottman.com

Gillian Sandstom, The Sussex Centre for Research on Kindness: gilliansandstrom.com

Erin Peavey, design researcher and architect: erinpeavey.com

Dr Aric Sigman, author and PSHE Health Education lecturer: aricsigman.com

Youaligned, mobility exercises: Youaligned.com

Ploenchan 'Mook' Vinyaratn, artist-designer, online bazaar: mookv.com

Qualy, design for a better world: qualydesign.com

Dr Robert Waldinger, American psychiatrist, psychoanalyst and Zen priest: robertwaldinger.com

United for all Ages, tackling loneliness, ageism, care, health, housing and learning: unitedforallages.com

Yesim Kunter, play expert: playtoinnovate.com

Tourism Authority of Thailand: tourismthailand.org

Magic of Thailand, UK Thai festivals: magicofthailand.co.uk

Kat Talks Thai, learn Thai the fun way with videos on TikTok and Instagram (@Kattalkstai): kattalksthai.com

Wor. Watthana Muay Thai Gym: worwatthana.com

Eloise Skinner, author, existential therapist, teacher: eloiseskinner.com; @eloiseallexia

Jessamy Hibberd, chartered clinical psychologist: drjessamy.com

Noel McDermott, psychotherapist, founder of Mental Health Works and The Wellbeing Show podcast: mentalhealthworks.net

Action for Happiness, promoting a happier and more caring society: actionforhappiness.org

Mind: mind.org.uk/workplace/mental-health-at-work/five-ways-to-wellbeing

Kattalin Buasrichan, Thai massage therapist and trainer: thaitherapymassage.co.uk

Further Sources

p.9   visa.co.th/en_TH/partner-with-us/market-insights/word-on-the-street.html

p.30   Nawijn J., Marchand M.A., Veenhoven R. and Vingerhoets A.J., 'Vacationers happier, but most not happier after a holiday'. *Applied Research in Quality of Life*. 2010 5(1):35–47. Doi: 10.1007/s11482-009-9091-9

p.31   news.ucmerced.edu/news/2015/relax-benefits-leisure-go-beyond-moment

p.36   Van Boven, L. and Gilovich, T., 'To do or to have? That is the question'. *Journal of Personality and Social Psychology. 2003 85*(6), 1193–1202. Doi: 10.1037/0022-3514.85.6.1193

Lyubomirsky, S., 'Hedonic adaptation to positive and negative experiences'. In *The Oxford Handbook of Stress, Health, and Coping* pp. 200–224 (Oxford University Press 2012)

p.48   Rizzolatti G. and Craighero L., 'The mirror-neuron system'. *Annual Review of Neuroscience*. 2004 27(1):169–192. Doi: 10.1146/annurev.neuro.27.070203.144230

p.50   Holmes, Henry and Tangtongtavy, Suchada, *Working With the Thais: A Guide to Managing in Thailand (*White Lotus Co, new edition 1997)

p.54   actionforhappiness.org/10-keys

p.59   McDool, Emily, Powell, Philip, Roberts, Jennifer and Taylor, Karl B., 'Social media use and children's wellbeing'. *IZA Discussion Paper* No. 10412. Doi: 10.2139/ssrn.2886783

p.66   bbc.co.uk/news/technology-28677674

p.67   Rosen, Christine, 'The myth of multitasking: how intentional self-distraction hurts us'. *The New Atlantis*, 2008 20:105–110. thenewatlantis.com/publications/the-myth-of-multitasking

p.68   Verduyn, Philippe, 'Not all bad: social media also have a positive impact on mental health'. *Maastricht University*. 17 August 2023. maastrichtuniversity.nl/news/not-all-bad-social-media-also-have-positive-impact-mental-health

p.69   data.ai/en/go/state-of-mobile-2022/

Majid, Aisha, 'Most popular news sources in the UK'. *Press Gazette*. 20 July 2023. pressgazette.co.uk/media-audience-and-business-data/most-popular-news-sources-uk-tiktok-ofcom-news-consumption-survey/

p.71   Brailovskaia, J., Delveaux, J., John, J., Wicker, V., Noveski, A., Kim, S., Schillack, H. and Margraf, J., 'Finding the "sweet spot" of smartphone use: reduction or abstinence to increase well-being and healthy lifestyle? An experimental intervention study'. *Journal of Experimental Psychology Applied, 2023 29(*1):149–161. Doi: 0.1037/xap0000430

p.72   He J-w., Tu Z-h., Xiao L., Su T. and Tang Y-x., 'Effect of restricting bedtime mobile phone use on sleep, arousal, mood, and working memory: A randomized pilot trial'. *PLoS ONE*, 2020 15(2). Doi: 10.1371/journal.pone.0228756

p.80   Mineo, Liz, 'Harvard study, almost 80 years old, has proved that embracing community helps us live longer, and be happier'. *The Harvard Gazette* 11 April 2017. news.harvard.edu/gazette/story/2017/04/over-nearly-80-years-harvard-study-has-been-showing-how-to-live-a-healthy-and-happy-life/

p.83   Branson, Adam, 'Is multi-generational living the future of housing?' *RICS. org*. 1 March 2020. ww3.rics.org/uk/en/modus/built-environment/homes-and-communities/all-together-now--mult-igenerational-living.html

p.87   Holt-Lunstad J., Smith T.B. and Layton J.B., 'Social relationships and mortality risk: a meta-analytic review'. *PLoS Medicine* 2010 7(7). Doi: 10.1371/journal.pmed.1000316

p.89   Boothby, E. J., Cooney, G., Sandstrom, G. M. and Clark, M. S., 'The Liking Gap in conversations: do people like us more than we think?' *Psychological Science*, 2018 29(11), 1742–1756. Doi: 10.1177/0956797618783714

p.105   gottman.com/blog/the-magic-relationship-ratio-according-science/

p.109   Sandstrom, G. M. and Dunn, E. W., 'Social interactions and well-being: the surprising power of weak ties'. *Personality and Social Psychology Bulletin*, 2014 40(7), 910-922. Doi: 10.1177/0146167214529799

p.112   gov.uk/government/news/pm-commits-to-government-wide-drive-to-tackle-loneliness

        bbc.co.uk/mediacentre/latestnews/2018/loneliest-age-group-radio-4

p.113   thetimes.co.uk/article/stuart-andrew-it-wasn-t-easy-to-admit-i-was-lonely-zn0pl86jg

p.122   2013 by UnitedHealth Group; unitedhealthgroup.com/newsroom/2017/0914studydoinggoodisgoodforyou.html

p.126   Richards, Serena, 'Kaz Crossley: heritage, inspirations and good vibes' *PWR Magazine*, 17 August 2022. https://www.pwrmagazine.com/post/kaz-crossley-heritage-inspirations-and-good-vibes

p.144   changingminds.org/disciplines/psychoanalysis/concepts/good-enough_mother.htm

p.147   psychcentral.com/news/2018/05/15/too-many-extracurricular-activities-for-kids-may-do-more-harm-than-good#1v

p.158   Pathike, Wilaiwan, O'Brien, Anthony Paul and Hunter, Sharyn, 'Moving on from adversity: an understanding of resilience in rural Thai older people'. *Aging & Mental Health*, 2019 23:3, 311–318, Doi: 10.1080/13607863.2017.1411883

p.174   Carr, Priyanka B. and Walton, Gregory M., 'Cues of working together fuel intrinsic motivation'. *Journal of Experimental Social Psychology,* 2014 53:169–184. Doi 10.1016/j.jesp.2014.03.015.v

p.186   mind.org.uk/workplace/mental-health-at-work/five-ways-to-wellbeing

p.230   University of Hertfordshire. 'Happiness: it's not in the jeans'. *ScienceDaily*. 8 March 2012. sciencedaily.com/releases/2012/03/120308062537.htm.

p.240   mirror.co.uk/lifestyle/food-drink/recipes/top-dinner-party-hosting-stress-30769054

Picture Credits

Acknowledgements

Thanks to family and friends for their patience while I locked myself away to write this book, and for keeping me motivated when the spirit of sanuk was lacking at my desk.

Much love to Sit for his loyalty, encouragement and constant supply of delicious food, but especially for showing me the real Thailand, then leaving it behind to brave so many British winters. To Siam for being the best son, and his girlfriend Chloe, whose design vision was invaluable, as was that of the legend that is Andy Luckett. I'm grateful to my Thai family for welcoming me and ensuring my time in the Land of Smiles is always sanuk.

Many thanks to my agent Jemima and editor Cyan for their enthusiasm from the start, and to editor Julia for her unflappability. Joanna Cooke at Departure PR, Nat at Frog & Wolf and Lee at Dynamic PR all played a huge role in the creation of this book, as did the Tourist Authority of Thailand. Khop Khun Ka.

Special thanks to two mates who love Thailand as much as I do – Jane, my travelling companion on that first life-changing trip, and Fuzz, whose beach conversations last year inspired me to spread the sanuk word. To cheerleading old friends (Paul, Julia, Debbi and Paul); Chat girls; Hearst Lifestylers, especially Team Prima (Jo, Jo, Andy and Sandra), and our sweary coven of brilliance (Jackie, Megan and Tash).

Finally, love to my sisters – Jackie, Lesli, Claire – and to Pam and John, for being there during the toughest of times. I'd like to dedicate this to my much-missed mum, Pat.